"HOW DO I GET THESE KIDS TO LISTEN?"

"HOW DO I GET THESE KIDS TO LISTEN?"

Practical Ways to Gain and Hold Attention in the Classroom

By
Evangelist Ed Dunlop

Illustrated by
Rebecca Dunlop

P. O. BOX 1099, MURFREESBORO, TN 37133

Printed and Bound in the United States of America

CONTENTS

Introduction i

1. The Positive Power of Proper Preparation............................1

2. The Virtue, Value and Validity of a Variety of Visuals 23

3. Balloon Bust Boards and Other Beneficial Behavior Boons 57

4. Cluttered Classrooms Cause Confusion and Chaos 79

5. Everyone Enjoys Energetic, Excited Enthusiasm 95

6. Storytelling Sets the Stage for Sweet Success............................111

7. Putting the Persuasive Power of Pupil Participation
   Into Practice 129

8. The Verifiable Value of Visitation................................147

9. Reaping Rich Relationships 165

10. Dealing With Defiant Dudes (and Dudesses)............................181

11. The Power of Prevailing Prayer..201

    A Final Word 211

    About the Author 215

INTRODUCTION

The second buzzer sounded, signaling the end of the Sunday school hour at Calvary Baptist Church. Tim Wellington turned to his wife, Lisa. "Better hurry, Sweetheart," he said. "We don't want to be late for our first day in Children's Church."

He strode toward the door, clutching his Bible and a time-worn puppet, while Lisa scooped up a large packet of Children's Church curriculum materials and hurried to catch up.

Mrs. Peabody blocked the aisle. A member of the Young Married Class for more than forty years, she had refused to be promoted to another adult class, even though her youngest son was now too old for the class. "Lisa, darling," she crooned, "your special last Sunday was simply divine! I just love to hear you sing!"

"Thank you, Mrs. Peabody. I'm thankful that the Lord used it," Lisa answered.

"In my opinion, they should have you sing every Sunday," the elderly lady went on, oblivious to the fact that other class members were attempting to squeeze past her. "Your music touches my heart every time."

Lisa managed a weak smile. "Thank you."

Tim grabbed her elbow. "Come on, Lisa; we gotta be going."

Lisa nodded and turned to the elderly saint. "Excuse us, please, Mrs. Peabody," she said, "but we're in a bit of a hurry. It's our first Sunday in Children's Church."

Mrs. Peabody seemed not to hear. Blocking Lisa's only avenue of escape, she chattered away for several minutes while Tim impatiently stewed. Finally, he grabbed Lisa's arm and literally dragged her past the dear lady. "Sorry to run out like this, Mrs. Peabody," he explained, "but Lisa and I have to go! We'll catch you later."

Tim and Lisa hurried eagerly toward the Children's Church classroom. "This is something I've always wanted to do," Tim declared. "I'm glad Pastor asked us to teach."

Lisa glanced toward the door of the classroom. "Sounds like they're killing each other!"

The Wellingtons paused in the doorway, silently surveying the tumultuous Children's Church classroom. "Uh-oh," Tim muttered.

The room was a scene of noisy disorder as thirty-some elementary children waited unattended. Several boys were playing football in the aisle, using a hymnal in place of the customary pigskin. At the chalkboard, four or five girls were scribbling furiously, pausing from time to time to try to erase each other's artwork. A cacophony of sound issued from the piano as two boys and a girl pounded on the keys and fought over the privilege of pumping the foot pedals. A few kids sat quietly, but one or two of the younger ones were in tears. A thin-faced boy sat in the corner, busily making airplanes from gospel tracts.

Feelings of apprehension swept over Tim as he stepped into the room. "Everybody, take your seat!" he called in the most authoritative voice he could muster. "Time for Children's Church to begin."

The trio on the piano paused just long enough to decide that Tim didn't pose too much of a threat, then went back to their pounding. The football game continued without interruption. A gospel airplane sailed past Tim's head.

Tim raised his voice. "Get quiet!" he shouted. "I mean it! Now get in your seats!" He was taken by surprise at his own angry outburst; but at least the discord on the piano ceased, the football game dissolved, and the kids sullenly took their seats.

"We're Mr. and Mrs. Wellington," he said, struggling to sound cheerful and friendly. "We're going to be your new Children's Church teachers."

Most of the kids looked at the floor, but the few who did meet his gaze returned it with icy stares. Tim swallowed hard. *This isn't gonna be as easy as we thought*, he told himself. *What have we gotten ourselves into?*

Seventy-five exasperating minutes later, the kids made a beeline for the door. A variety of emotions overwhelmed Tim as he gratefully watched them go: helpless frustration at knowing that he and Lisa had not done a very good job, anger at the kids for being so unruly, guilt for feeling such anger, and a growing sense of dread as he realized that he and Lisa would face the same horrendous situation again next Sunday.

"It's just not going to work out," he told Lisa as she tossed the teaching materials into the back seat of the Lexus, then slid in beside him. "I guess we just didn't know what we were getting into."

Lisa slammed the car door, then let out a long sigh. Tim glanced over at her and realized that she was close to tears. "But we both felt that God was in it," she whispered. "You and I both were thrilled when Pastor asked us to do it. I think we should try it again next week. Maybe we'll do better. At least we have a better idea of what to expect."

Tim started the car and jammed it into reverse. "But these kids were little monsters!" he exploded. "Four fights during the one service! One four-year-old wet his pants, and one girl made seven trips to the bathroom—I counted! And those two little girls on the second row never did quit talking and giggling. There was so much talking and cutting up and shuffling of chairs that I don't think the kids heard a single word of the lesson. It was like trying to teach at a hockey game! Lisa, I don't think I can take another Sunday of this!"

Lisa sighed. "It didn't turn out the way I expected either," she admitted. "And I was really looking forward to teaching these kids!"

The Lexus eased out into traffic. "I'm gonna call Pastor Rogers this afternoon," Tim promised. "I'll tell him the Children's Church thing just isn't gonna work. He'll have all this week to find somebody else."

Perhaps your introduction to teaching wasn't as rough as Tim and Lisa's, but classroom discipline is a problem that every children's teacher faces at one time or another.

It's a constant challenge to try to hold the attention of today's children. We're working with a generation of children who, for the most part, were raised on TV and video games; kids who are unruly and undisciplined; kids who tell their own parents what to do and get away with it!

And whoso shall receive one such little child in my name receiveth me.
Matthew 18:5

They saunter into our Sunday school and Junior Church classrooms virtually unable to sit still, unwilling to follow orders, and unable to concentrate for more than just a few moments. They're accustomed to "doing their own thing."

Even so it is not the will of your Father which is in heaven, that one of these little ones should perish.
Matthew 18:14

Yet these same disorderly, disobedient and defiant children are desperate for love. The majority of your students (including many of your "church kids") will be from broken homes. Many of them see themselves as unloved and unwanted. What a ministry to be able to introduce them to Jesus, the One who loved them and died for them!

And all thy children shall be taught of the LORD; and great shall be the peace of thy children.
Isaiah 54:13

This past week I was reading a book by a veteran children's evangelist. In discussing the needs of America's children, he stated, "And this is a day that is so full of hustle and bustle that many are growing up starved for the affection that is their due. Especially is this true in recent years when the changing scene has brought such a change in the homelife of the family." In a later chapter he writes, "The last few decades have witnessed the deterioration of the home."

I turned to the copyright page and found that the book was published in 1948! Imagine what this writer would say about the American home today!

Tim walked into the kitchen to hang up the cordless phone, then turned to Lisa who was loading the dishwasher. "Pastor's not home," he said. "I've tried three times. I'll guess we'll just have to tell him at church tonight, but I hate to do it face-to-face."

Lisa brushed a wisp of blond hair out of her blue eyes as she turned to face him. "Tim," she said softly, "I've been thinking. Maybe the Lord doesn't want us to quit so soon. Maybe that's why you can't get hold of Pastor. Why don't we try it just one more week?"

Tim let out his breath in a long sigh. "Honey, I don't think I can take another Sunday like today. Those kids are impossible! They don't need a teacher—they need a prison guard!"

Lisa's eyes filled with tears. "That may be where some of those kids are heading unless someone like us can reach them for the Lord Jesus."

Tim had no answer.

"Why not call Larry Edwards?" Lisa suggested. "He and Debbie have taught the kids at their church for several years, and they seem to really love it. Maybe they can give us some pointers."

> **For God is not unrighteous to forget your work and labour of love, which ye have shewed toward his name, in that ye have ministered to the saints, and do minister.**
> **Hebrews 6:10**

We're not going to allow Tim and Lisa to quit just yet. We're going to send them some help. They're going to learn how to gain and hold the attention of today's children, how to develop caring relationships with their students, and how to eliminate most of the discipline problems before they even start. They're going to be pleasantly surprised to discover that they are both far more creative than they ever dreamed possible. They're going to find out for themselves that teaching can be a joyous, rewarding experience.

As they learn and grow and increase their effectiveness in their children's ministry, I trust that you'll learn and grow in your own teaching ministry for the Lord.

Sunday school teachers are special people!

So why do you teach children?

___Pastor asked me, and I just couldn't say "no."

___The superintendent asked me, and I just...

✓ I love kids.

✓ I'm deeply moved and motivated by Matthew 18:14 and 19:14.

✓ I believe that children have eternal souls.

✓ If I don't teach them, who will?

✓ I'm preparing for a more important ministry with the adults, but I figure I can use the experience with the kids.

___They'll mention it in my obituary.

___I have kids of my own.

___God called me.

___No one else would take the class.

___My wife/husband talked me into it.

___I have a lot of time on my hands now that the grandkids have moved away.

___I enjoy teaching.

Check the reasons that apply to you.

Will it matter in eternity?

Imagine yourself in eternity, walking down the golden streets, enjoying the presence of the Lord Jesus and the songs of the redeemed. Your mind goes back to your earthly life, and the year 1996 in particular. Which of the following events and achievements will really matter to you then?

___Shaquille O'Neal signed a $120 million contract to play basketball with the L.A. Lakers.

___I was able to purchase a new Windstar minivan.

___Seven children received Christ as Saviour in my class.

___My son's soccer team won the league championship.

___I was faithful in my service to God.

___The United States won 44 gold medals at the 1996 Olympics.

___My daughter made the honor roll at school.

___A boy in my class surrendered his life to the Lord. He later went to the mission field and won hundreds of souls to Jesus.

___I gave $1,200 to missions, and my sacrifice helped reach the lost.

___I put in enough overtime to get myself promoted to office manager.

___I won my own son to the Lord.

___I watched 780 hours of television.

Put your emphasis on the things that matter!

10 Reasons to Quit Teaching

If you are considering quitting your class, check any reason(s) below that apply to you:

__ 1. **No one appreciates the many hours I put in for my class.**

__ 2. **My students are so rowdy—I can't take it anymore.**

__ 3. **I'm extremely busy and just don't have time for proper preparation.**

__ 4. **I've lost my burden for the kids.**

__ 5. **I don't think I'm accomplishing anything worthwhile.**

__ 6. **I'm beginning to doubt that God really called me to teach.**

__ 7. **My nerves can't handle the noise.**

__ 8. **The church is not really behind my ministry: I can't get needed supplies and equipment.**

__ 9. **I hear more criticism than praise.**

__10. **Other** _____

10 Reasons to Stay Faithful

If God called you to teach, quitting your class would be a major mistake. Consider the following reasons to stay:

__ 1. **God is not unrighteous to forget my work and labor of love (Heb. 6:10).**

__ 2. **By reading this book, I can learn to improve the discipline in my classroom.**

__ 3. **I can learn to manage my time and reconsider my priorities, creating time for ministry.**

__ 4. **God can renew my burden for the eternal souls in my class.**

__ 5. **The results are up to God; often I'm touching lives in ways I cannot see.**

__ 6. **God is using me for His glory.**

__ 7. **I'm going to develop a close relationship with each of my students and learn how to captivate their attention.**

__ 8. **I'm serving God, and I can find ways to obtain needed materials.**

__ 9. **They criticized Jesus too.**

__10. **Jesus is coming soon!**

1.

THE POSITIVE POWER OF PROPER PREPARATION

Tim Wellington and Larry Edwards had worked together for several years as jet engine mechanics at Delta Air Lines. Larry was a faithful member of another fundamental Baptist church in town, and when each had discovered that the other was a believer, they became fast friends. For several years they had taken lunch breaks together, and they always enjoyed fellowshipping with one another.

When Tim had come up for a promotion a few months earlier, he had managed to get himself transferred to Larry's department. Now the two men worked side by side in the same work station, rebuilding gearboxes that transferred power from the jet engines to the auxiliary equipment on the aircraft.

Tim picked up the phone again, rapidly punched in seven digits, then held the receiver to his ear. "Larry's probably not even home now," he muttered.

"Hello." Larry's voice was crisp and businesslike, yet conveyed warmth and friendliness.

"Larry, this is Tim. How's it going?"

"Just great, Tim. We had a good service today in Children's Church."

Tim smiled ruefully. *Wish I could say the same*, he thought. "That's what I wanted to talk to you about," he said. "Lisa and I just took the Children's Church here at Calvary."

"Tim, that's great!" Larry exclaimed. "How'd it go?"

"Lousy," Tim blurted. "Larry, these kids are a bunch of juvenile delinquents! It was a circus in there! I want to tell Pastor that we're just not cut out for teaching, but Lisa thinks we should give it another go."

"Does God want you in there?"

1

"I felt like He did until today," Tim admitted, "but now I'm not sure. I can't take another day like today!"

"What age group do you have?" Larry asked.

"Four-year-olds through sixth grade. It was too big a group, and it just didn't work."

"Is there anyone who would take the four- and five-year-olds in another class?"

"Probably," Tim replied. "It would be a smaller, easier group."

"Discuss it with your pastor," Larry suggested. "If you have four-year-olds through sixth grade, that's an age span of eight or nine years. It just doesn't work. There's more difference between a four-year-old and a sixth grader than there is between a third grader and a college student. Get your pastor to divide the group and get a teacher for the fours and fives."

"But it's still too big a group," Tim protested. "Even with the little guys gone, we would still have about thirty kids!"

"We had 127 in our Children's Church at Faith this morning," Larry said quietly.

Tim was astonished. "A hundred and...you gotta be kidding! How'd it go?"

"Fine, fine," Larry answered. "The Lord gave us a great service, and four kids were saved. It was a good day."

"Maybe you can give us some pointers," Tim said. "Lisa and I can really use some help."

"Have you ever taught before?"

"Uh-uh," Tim replied. "We've only been saved five or six years. We got saved just after we were married."

"Are they giving you any help or training?"

"Not really. Pastor just gave us a packet of lesson materials and one dirty, old puppet and told us to go to it. I *suppose* they'll help us if we have problems or questions."

Larry sighed. "I'm afraid it's that way in most fundamental churches, especially in the children's departments," he said. "We have the most important task in the world, yet we approach it in a very haphazard manner."

"Hey, am I interrupting anything important?" Tim asked. "I didn't get you up from your Sunday afternoon nap or anything, did I?"

His friend laughed. "The nap comes later. I was just sitting down to study my Children's Church lesson when the phone rang."

"Children's Church lesson?" Tim echoed. "You mean, like, for next Sunday?"

"Sure."

"But Sunday's a whole week away!"

"Preparation is the key to effective teaching," Larry answered quietly. "That's usually where the battle is won or lost. The earlier you start studying, the better job you do."

"But Sunday is a whole week away!" Tim repeated.

"Early preparation is the best," Larry said. "The teacher who waits until Saturday night is not giving the Lord his best. When you start early in the week, the needs of your students are fresh in your mind. You have time to study, to meditate on the lesson, and to gather any materials you need. You can pray over the lesson all week. No more 'Saturday Night Specials' for me!"

"I didn't even look through the lesson materials until Saturday evening," Tim admitted. "I just thought that was the way it was done."

"Often that is the way it's done, but it's not the right way," Larry retorted. "Hey, listen, let's discuss this at work tomorrow. We're tearing down the gearbox from that 767, and the first two or three hours we'll just be cleaning parts. You and I could do that in our sleep! It'll be a good opportunity to talk about our children's ministries. I'll give you all the help I can."

"Thanks, Larry. I...I think we'll hold off calling Pastor Rogers. See you tomorrow."

Lisa returned to the kitchen just as Tim hung up the phone. "So what did Larry have to say?"

Tim shook his head in disbelief. "They had 127 kids in Junior Church today," he replied, "and Larry said that things went

smoothly! Can you believe that? Whatever he has, we could sure use some of it!"

Larry Edwards is right. Preparation is the key to effectively teaching God's Word, whether you're teaching toddlers or senior saints. The teacher who goes into class without adequate preparation has already failed before the teaching hour even starts. It's been said that the teacher who fails to prepare, prepares to fail.

PREPARATION IS THE KEY TO EFFECTIVE TEACHING

Teaching the Word of God to boys and girls is the most important job you will ever do in your entire life. Other than raising your own children to serve God, nothing else compares in significance to teaching. How dare we give less than our best! How dare we walk into class unprepared!

Show me a teacher who has an orderly, attentive class, and I'll show you a teacher who is well prepared. Show me a teacher who has discipline problems, and I'll show you a teacher who has not taken the time for proper preparation.

PREPARE EARLY IN THE WEEK!

The key to effective teaching is thorough preparation. There are no shortcuts.

The very first step in preparing for class is to prepare your own heart. Go to your knees in prayer, confessing any and all sin. Make sure you are right with God. Ask God for His wisdom and guidance as you begin your study and preparation. Always remember that we are in a spiritual battle, and we must have God's power. How foolish the teacher who would attempt to teach dependent upon his own feeble wisdom and ability when the wisdom and power of the Almighty God are at his disposal! Seek God's face and ask His blessing on your preparations.

Continue your preparations for class by preparing the Bible lesson.

BE PREPARED!

It's the most important component of the teaching hour, and it requires the greatest amount of preparation. How strange that any teacher would spend more time and effort in preparing puppet skits, crafts, bus promotions, etc., than he does in Bible-lesson preparation!

Study the lesson. Start by reading the Scripture text for the lesson, studying it, meditating on it, and asking God to lead you as you seek to apply its truths to the lives of your students.

If the lesson is centered around a Bible story (nearly every lesson should be), read and reread the text of the story until it becomes real in your mind. Visualize the characters in your imagination. What do they look like? How do they talk? How would each react to the events in the story?

Divide the action into separate scenes and visualize the events in each scene. Practice narrating the story until you have the details down in proper sequence, then add dialogue, descriptions, and other details. Allow the story to move you emotionally as you work through it. On occasion, a story may move you to tears as you practice—then you know you're getting close to being ready.

The teacher who fails to prepare, prepares to fail!

Pray for wisdom as you seek to apply the lesson to the lives of your students. Always remember that any curriculum materials you may use were written by writers who have never met your students. Therefore, the teaching aim that they present in the lesson may or may not be the one that you will zero in on as you teach the lesson. Ask God for guidance.

Stories bring the lesson to life for your listeners; therefore, look for illustrations with which to open, apply and close your lesson. The wise teacher will seldom build an entire lesson around a modern-day, real-life illustration, but such stories are excellent to introduce a lesson topic and channel the interest toward the day's lesson. They also provide a means to bring a lesson to a close and apply the biblical truth to the everyday lives of the hearers.

A good story grabs the child's attention, conveys truth in an enjoyable, interesting way, and makes a lasting impression upon his heart.

You want to appeal to the sense of sight as well as the sense of hearing, so find a way to visualize your lesson for your students. Be sure to use visual aids for every part of the lesson, not just the Bible story. Isn't the application a vital part of the lesson? Should it not be visualized?

As you prepare the lesson, be alert to the attention-holding value of

Visual Aids Capture Attention!

each aspect of your teaching. Does the opening illustration grab your interest, focusing your attention on the lesson? If not, why use it? Why not find a more interesting, more appropriate one? Rest assured that if the story does not "grab" you, it will certainly not "grab" your Primaries and Juniors.

> **Interest leads to attention; attention leads to learning.**

Are the visual aids attractive and interesting? If not, then find another way to visualize the truth at hand.

Your lesson preparation is a key to your success as a teacher, and yet so many teachers fall down in this vital area. Poor preparation produces ineffective teaching.

When you walk into class on Sunday, your lesson should be so well studied, so "prayed over," so well prepared that you can teach it without a single glance at the lesson manual. In fact, your students shouldn't even know that such a book exists! Prepare your lesson so thoroughly that it excites you, overwhelms you, and becomes so compelling that you feel you will die if you are not allowed to share it with your students!

Once the Bible lesson is studied and prepared, begin work on the other aspects of your program. If you are the one responsible for leading songs during the teaching hour, you should walk into class with every song chosen in advance, sheet music prepared for your piano player, and the visualized songs ready to go. Prepare the memory verse, the missionary story, the Bible review game, etc., long before class time.

Woe to the teacher who rushes into class three minutes before starting time, grabs a songbook, and starts paging frantically through it! Even worse is the song

Kids like VARIETY, and they like ACTIVITIES that get them involved.

Lack of preparation leads to lack of control.

leader who saunters up to stand before the children and drawls, "Ah…what do you all want to sing?" Be prepared!

If all this sounds like work, you're right. It is work, but every moment spent in preparation for class pays tremendous dividends the instant you walk into the classroom!

The teacher who fails to prepare is planning to fail.

"So how much time do you spend each week in lesson preparation?" Tim asked as he selected a socket from his toolbox. "This sounds like a lot of work!"

"It is work," Larry agreed. "And it takes time. I try to spend a minimum of four hours on lesson preparation each week."

"Four hours!" Tim exclaimed. "You're kidding!"

Larry shook his head. "It's worth it, Tim. Look at it this way: I had 127 students for an hour and a quarter yesterday. Multiply 127 by one and a quarter, and you have over 158 student hours! If I spend 240 minutes in lesson preparation, they're collectively spending over 9,500 minutes listening to me!"

Tim shook his head. "It doesn't seem like all that much when you put it that way."

"And look at it another way," Larry went on. "Four kids got saved yesterday. What's four hours compared with four eternities?"

Using power nut drivers, the two men removed the gears from the housing, then began to tear down the unit. Larry glanced across at Tim. "So what happened in your Children's Church? You said that things didn't go very well."

"That's the understatement of the year," Tim replied. "The kids were talking and giggling and cutting up throughout the entire program! I felt like we never really had their attention! But I'm not quite sure what to do to improve things."

"Describe your program to me."

"Huh?"

"You had over an hour with the kids, right? What happened during that time? How much time did you spend singing? How long was the lesson? How did you plan the time?"

Tim thought for a moment. "I guess we sang for twenty or twenty-five minutes, then took about five minutes for prayer requests. Lisa worked with the kids for about five minutes on a memory verse, then I did the lesson. Then I guess we had about fifteen minutes of singing after the lesson."

"Not much variety," Larry commented.

"Hey, it was the best we could do!" Tim shot back, a hurt look on his face. "It was our first time!"

His friend held up one hand apologetically. "Tim, I'm not being critical. I'm here to help. But Primaries and Juniors need action, variety, a change of pace. They need a fast-paced program that holds their attention, gets them involved and keeps things moving."

Tim looked puzzled. "But how do we do that?"

Larry placed three nuts in the parts tray, then grimaced as he struggled to pull an oil nozzle free. "Look at the schedule you just shared with me," he said. "You had the kids sing for twenty or twenty-five minutes, then prayer time took five minutes, and the memory verse probably took another five. Then, what, twenty minutes for the lesson?"

Tim nodded.

"After that you had the kids sing for another fifteen minutes."

"So what's wrong with that?" Tim blurted out.

Larry looked thoughtful. "How many times did you have the kids stand? Can you remember?"

"None, I guess."

"There's your very first problem," Larry said gently. "Your students sat for an hour and fifteen minutes without a chance to move around or change position. Wellington, even an adult would have a hard time sitting still that long."

Tim shrugged. "I guess you're right."

"And then," Larry went on, "there wasn't much variety to capture the attention and stimulate the mind. You said that you sang for twenty or twenty-five minutes. The kids sat and listened to the Bible lesson for twenty minutes. You had another block of songs at the end that lasted for fifteen minutes. Tim, your program needs *variety*."

Tim looked puzzled. "So what should we have done?"

"Sword drills, Scripture puzzles, puppets and object lessons," Larry replied. "Filmstrips or videos, missionary stories, and especially Bible games. Kids like variety, and they like activities that get them involved."

"So the Children's Church program should be a bunch of fun stuff?"

"Not fun just for the sake of fun. Every part of your program should have a definite purpose and should tie in to the teaching aim for the day. If an activity doesn't teach or serve a definite purpose, throw it out.

"If you use a Sword drill, have the kids look up verses that apply to the day's lesson. Any object lesson you use should reinforce the teaching aim. Show a short video or filmstrip if it teaches the same truth as your Bible lesson; present a magic trick that does the same. Get your kids involved in an exciting lesson review by using a Bible game."

"What's a Bible game?" Tim wanted to know.

"It's a fantastic way to review by asking questions from the lesson, then letting the students who answer participate in a scoring game. Some of the games are played on the flannel board, and some use the overhead projector. We always play boys against girls, and the competition is awesome! I'll loan you one of our games before Sunday. Your class will love it!"

Tim was silent for several minutes as he immersed a collection of nuts, bolts and washers in a solution of parts cleaner. "So what you're saying," he finally said, "is that our discipline problems are the result of a lack of preparation? We didn't have enough variety in the program and didn't have enough student participation to hold their interest?"

Larry nodded as he dunked the oil nozzle in the solution. "That's a good part of it," he agreed. "You have to keep the kids interested, and that takes a lot of work and preparation. Interest is the key to attention, and attention leads to learning. You don't teach much without the attention of your pupils."

Tim laughed. "I guess you could say we learned that yesterday."

Larry lifted the nozzle out of the solution. "I need to throw this in the varsol tank for a few minutes," he said. "Remind me at lunch, and I'll sketch out the schedule we used yesterday in Children's Church. It will give you an idea of the variety we used in pacing our program."

As Larry Edwards said, interest is the key to attention, and attention leads to learning. It's an exercise in futility to try to teach unless you have the attention of your students.

If your students are bored, inattentive or disinterested, obviously some changes need to be made. Ask God to guide you as you seek to locate and correct the underlying causes of your students' disinterest.

Any teaching program for children, whether it be Sunday school or Children's Church, Master Clubs, AWANA, Vacation Bible School or Junior Camp, should incorporate a variety of teaching methods and activities. A fast-paced program that presents the biblical truth in a variety of ways, employs lots of action and visuals, and utilizes student involvement is sure to hold the interest and attention of your students.

You must have the attention of your class in order for effective learning to take place. It takes work, but you can do it!

Again, one of the most important keys to holding the attention of children is to use variety. In scheduling your teaching hour, don't plan long periods of class time that drag out one single activity. Never schedule fifteen or twenty or twenty-five minutes of singing in one block of time. Your students will become tired of it, lose interest and turn their attention elsewhere.

Instead, plan five minutes of singing (three songs?). Have the students stand for the first song, sit for the next, stand again for the third, etc. Keep those kids moving! Then present a captivating missionary story. Have two or three more songs, then drill the memory verse. Use a short, lively puppet skit, then collect the offering. Have the students stand for another song, then involve them in a Scripture puzzle. Any program for kids should be fast-paced, with lots of variety, action, and student involvement.

Tim and Larry sat in the non-smoking section of the employee cafeteria, their lunches temporarily forgotten. Larry was using a Magic Marker to sketch out a class schedule on a full sheet of white

paper, writing so large as to be legible from fifteen feet away.

"Here's a rough idea of the schedule we followed yesterday in Children's Church," he told Tim. "I always write out my teaching schedule in large letters like this, then tape it to the table where I have my visuals. It's a simple way to keep the program on schedule with no lags or interruptions. Each of my workers who has a platform part that day also has a copy of the same schedule so he or she knows exactly when his or her part comes in."

Tim was amazed. "Do you always stay exactly on schedule?" he asked.

Larry shrugged. "Not always to the minute. The schedule is just a guide, and it has to be flexible, but you can make adjustments as the program takes place. For instance, yesterday we started about four minutes late because two of the Sunday school classes had a missionary speaker, and he dismissed late. I made up for the late start by dropping one of the opening songs, shortening the Sword drill, and dropping another song just before the message. When I started the Bible message, I was within a minute of being back on schedule."

Tim studied the sheet of paper. "You go right from one activity to the next, don't you? None of these goes for more than just a few minutes—well, except for the lesson. Wow! You taught for twenty-five minutes?"

Larry nodded.

"Did you hold their attention?"

He nodded again. "But even the message incorporated a variety of teaching methods. I opened with an interesting story, then had the kids read three text verses that I had visualized with the overhead projector. Then I went into about a twelve-minute Bible story, which was visualized with objects, giant flannelgraph and flashcards. After the Bible story I used three kids to role-play a situation to make the lesson application, then closed with another brief illustration. True, they sat for twenty-five minutes during the lesson, but there was a good deal of variety, and their attention was keen the entire time."

"And the Bible game took fifteen minutes?"

"Well, more like twelve. The invitation went just a little longer than I had planned. The Bible game is an exciting time of student involvement, and you seldom lose their attention. A review game gets the entire group participating."

Larry's schedule looked something like this:

Children's Church Schedule	
11:00	Fun Opener, Flag Salutes, Prayer
11:05	Songs
	1. This Is the Day
	2. If You're Saved
	3. Seek Ye First
11:10	Sword Drill
11:15	Offering
	Song (Favorite)
11:20	Puppet Song
	Song—I'll Be a Witness
11:25	Object Lesson
11:30	Songs
	1. Did You Ever
	2. More Than Gold
11:35	LESSON
	Invitation
12:00	Bible Game
12:15	Let's Make a Deal
12:20	Dismissal

"I think I see where some of our problems lie," Tim said, laying down the schedule and picking up his turkey sandwich. "We're certainly not this organized, and we surely didn't have this much variety in the program. Hey, I'm glad for your help, Edwards! If you don't mind, I'm gonna use some of your ideas."

Larry grinned. "Glad to be of service, Wellington. I hope some of these ideas will help you get things smoothed out in your Children's Church. It's pretty frustrating to try to teach if you don't have the attention of the kids."

Tim nodded. "We found that out!"

"While we're on the subject of preparation, let me mention one more thing. Always arrive early. Try to get there before the first kid and get things set up ahead of time."

Tim grinned sheepishly. "We blew it there too, thanks in part to Mrs. Peabody. The other couple that works with us were even later than us. I think next Sunday we'll sit in the back of the Young Married Class and leave about three minutes before the second buzzer. Maybe the Andersons will do the same."

"Do any Sunday school classes meet in your Children's Church room?"

"One—third grade, I think."

"Well, you can still set up some of your visuals and stuff before Sunday school," Larry advised, "as long as they're not in the other teacher's way. Then be waiting at the door, and as soon as the teacher dismisses the class, zip right in there and be ready. One of you can be setting up while the others talk quietly with the kids and keep order. Once all the classes are in, get off to a good, exciting start. It's so important to start smoothly."

Tim looked at his watch. "Hey! We'd better get to eating! Lunch break is nearly over!"

Larry laughed. "Lead us in prayer, won't you? Then I'll shut up and let you eat."

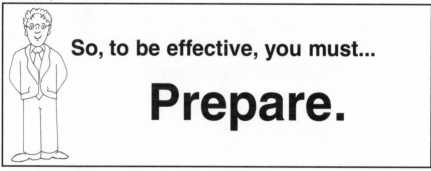

So, to be effective, you must...

Prepare.

Perry Pedagogue

I still remember the gift my brother Paul and I got for our dad one Father's Day. It was a tiny .22 caliber revolver with a one-and-a-half-inch barrel. The cylinder was so short it would only take .22 shorts—no longs or long rifles. The undersized handgrips were made of plastic, and the weapon was small enough for the average man to conceal in his hand. But the best part was the price—we only paid twelve dollars. We knew we had a bargain!

Paul and I accompanied Dad one afternoon as he went out to the Arizona desert to test-fire the thing. Click, click, boom! Click, boom! Click, click, click, boom! The hammer came down on the firing pin with so little force that the gun fired only every third or fourth shot. As a weapon for self-defense, that tiny revolver would have been almost useless. (It was about as reliable and trustworthy as a liberal politician.) It turned out that we had bought what's known as a "Saturday Night Special."

I only remember Dad's firing the revolver that one afternoon. He took it home and hid it away in a drawer, and I don't remember ever seeing it again. Looking back, I suppose he recognized just how useless and potentially dangerous our gift could be.

What a bargain! After all, it only cost us twelve dollars, but it could have cost Dad his life!

The "Saturday Night Special"

Cheaply made handgun   **Poorly prepared lesson**

1. Costs very little—can be obtained cheaply.	1. Costs the teacher very little time—no real sacrifice.
2. Very poor quality. Inferior materials and shoddy workmanship.	2. Ineffective lesson resulting from shoddy study habits, lack of concern, lack of prayer.
3. Usually inaccurate when fired.	3. Often biblically inaccurate.
4. Dangerous to user and others.	4. Detrimental to teacher and students.
5. Small, easily concealed.	5. Never concealed from God.
6. Often used in crimes by persons too lazy to make a living by honest means.	6. Often used by teachers too lazy to study and properly prepare.
7. Outlawed in many states.	7. Should be outlawed in churches.

Reasons for lesson preparation early in the week:

1. You are able to evaluate the previous lesson accurately.

2. The needs and problems of your students are fresh in your mind.

3. You have plenty of time for proper study.

4. You are able to meditate on the lesson all week.

5. You have time to gather needed materials.

6. You have time to become acquainted with current pupil needs.

EVALUATING MY CLASS PREPARATION

YES   NO

____ ____ 1. Do I start my preparation early in the week?

____ ____ 2. Do I begin my preparation time with prayer?

____ ____ 3. Do I study the lesson from the Bible before I study any lesson manual?

____ ____ 4. Do I write out a specific teaching aim for the teaching hour?

____ ____ 5. Do I plan the other elements of class around that teaching aim?

____ ____ 6. Do I prepare early enough in the week so that I have time to gather the necessary teaching materials?

____ ____ 7. Do I meditate on the lesson throughout the week?

____ ____ 8. Do I pray for my class throughout the week?

____ ____ 9. Am I so well prepared that the program flows smoothly and holds the attention of the students?

____ ____ 10. Are my teaching materials set up and ready before the first student arrives?

Ask Andy!

Dear Andy,

I am an elementary schoolteacher with an extremely busy schedule during the week. I know it's important to prepare my Sunday school lesson early in the week, but with my hectic schedule, the first chance I have even to glance at my lesson manual is Friday night. Honestly!

Is there any way to improve my situation? I want to do the best job I can for the Lord.

Carrie Oakey

Dear Carrie,

I appreciate your desire to do your best in your Sunday school class. You're right—it's vital to prepare early in the week.

If your schedule prevents you from thorough preparation early in the week, at least take fifteen minutes to read through your lesson on Sunday afternoon or evening to acquaint yourself with the teaching aim and the lesson outline. Then you'll be able to meditate on the lesson from time to time during the week, thinking through appropriate illustrations, etc. When you begin your in-depth study and preparation on Friday and Saturday, your lesson will take shape much easier!

Your friend,

Andy

Dear Andy,

My wife and I teach Children's Church, and we love it! We have the Primaries and Juniors combined, with a total of about sixty kids.

The problem is this—the third-grade Sunday school teacher dismisses late every Sunday, so we never can start on time! The other kids get restless while we're waiting, and we get off to a rough start every time.

We've talked with the third-grade teacher, but she doesn't seem to care. Any suggestions?

Rick O'Shay

Dear Rick,

Don't wait for the third-grade class; start on time! Have one of your workers ready to meet the latecomers at the door and usher them to seats on the back row.

Once the third graders realize that they are always sitting in the back and that they are missing out on part of your program, they'll put pressure on their teacher to get dismissed on time.

Never penalize the on-timers by waiting for the latecomers.

For the kids,

Dear Andy,

What can I, as a pastor, do to help and encourage my Children's Church workers? I have a good staff of faithful children's workers, but I know that they, like everyone else, get discouraged from time to time.

On Sunday morning, as we have our adult service in the main auditorium, we tend to forget about the kids in the back room. Out of sight is out of mind. It's almost as if we have two different churches meeting in the same building each week.

I guess what bothers me most is this: most of our bus kids do not even know who I am! When I meet some of them in the hallway, they don't even know that I am their pastor!

How can I bring these two ministries closer together?

Reverend Fiddle D. D.

Dear Pastor Fiddle,

Thanks for writing. I'm delighted that you see the importance of the children's ministries.

There are several ways that pastors can encourage their workers, and children's workers in particular. Pray for them. Pray for them privately, and pray for their ministries from the pulpit. Mention the children's church ministries during the morning service. Send notes of appreciation from time to time, especially during times of extensive work and sacrifice, such as a spring or fall attendance campaign.

But perhaps the most tangible way to show that these ministries are important to you is by visiting the children's departments. Take a ten-minute "leave of absence" from the platform during the Sunday morning service and pop in on your Children's Church. (Give your workers advance notice; they have the teaching hour planned, and you don't want to throw them off schedule.)

Have a worker introduce you to the class, then spend a few minutes letting the children get to know you. You might share your testimony or teach a new missions chorus, tell an exciting missionary story, or even read an interesting missions prayer letter. Drill the month's memory verse. Share a church prayer request. Present an appropriate object lesson that reinforces the teaching aim for that day. Don't just walk in and ad lib; prepare something brief that will minister to the kids.

The fact that you care enough to walk away from the adult service and make an appearance in children's church will do wonders for your workers, and the children will get to know you as their pastor. If I were pastoring, I would visit my children's churches at least once every eight weeks on a regular basis.

For the kids,

Andy

P. S. Children's Church director— you might wish to show this letter to your pastor.

Dear Andy,

I've been teaching in Master Clubs for several years. I really enjoy working with the kids, but lately I find myself getting easily upset with them. If some kid starts goofing around or cutting up, I have a hard time controlling my temper. I find myself resenting the kids who cause trouble.

It didn't use to be this way. Any ideas as to why I'm resenting these kids, instead of loving them?

Polly C. Holder

Dear Polly,

You're not the only teacher who has experienced what you just described. It happens to a lot of us. Sometimes we see certain students as problems, rather than seeing their potential.

Ask God to help you see each of your students through the eyes of Jesus. He loves even the unlovely! Pray for your students daily, and pray especially hard for those who cause trouble in class. Ask the Lord to love them through you.

You need to be firm with the troublemakers and never allow them to stir things up in class so that the other students cannot learn. But always deal with your students in love. Again, learn to see the problem students as potential, not as problems.

For the kids,

Andy

2.

THE VIRTUE, VALUE AND VALIDITY OF A VARIETY OF VISUALS

One of the most effective ways to hold the attention of your class and therefore minimize discipline problems is to use visual aids. A good visual aid properly used will pique the students' curiosity, stimulate their interest, catch and hold their attention, and lead to life-changing learning.

Visual aids are powerful teaching tools. The teacher who attempts to teach God's Word without them is minimizing his own effectiveness, short-changing his students, and actually working harder than he has to! It's easier to hold the attention of five hundred students by using good visuals than it is to try to hold the attention of fifteen without them.

In short, visuals are effective!

Captivate the attention of your students by using **VISUALS**

Tim inserted his time card into the slot at the bottom of the time clock, then withdrew the card when he heard the machine stamp his time. He held his breath as he glanced at the blue imprint. "Whew!" he exclaimed. "Made it with a minute to spare!" He racked the card, then hurried toward his department.

Larry looked up as he entered the work bay. "Just a bit early, aren't you? You could have slept in a little longer!"

Tim made a face. "Okay, Mr. Company man," he responded. "I'm on time, aren't I?"

"Just promise me you won't make this kind of appearance Sunday morning in Children's Church," Larry teased. "You're gonna be early, remember?"

Tim nodded. "Hey, Lisa and I started our preparation for Children's Church last night. I studied my lesson and worked out a program schedule, and Lisa chose some songs that go along with the teaching aim."

Larry grinned. "Aren't you a bit out of character?"

"We're taking this teaching job seriously," Tim replied gravely. "We're determined to do our best. We spent some time praying that God will bless this next Sunday."

He plopped down on the stool beside his workbench and resumed work on a gear package. "Our teaching packet has some little pictures we're supposed to use to teach the lesson," he said, "but to me they're really rinky-dink. The pictures are really small, for one thing. And the instructions say to put cellophane tape on the back of each picture and stick it to a teaching chart as you present the lesson. It seems kinda hokey to me."

"They don't sound very impressive," Larry agreed. "What lesson are you teaching?"

"The Passover," Tim replied. "You know, the story of the lamb's blood on the doorpost on the night of Israel's escape from Egypt. I figured it's a good chance to present salvation by showing how the Passover pointed to Calvary."

His friend nodded. "Excellent! Sounds like you've been working on it."

"But I don't like the teaching pictures," Tim complained again. "They're so small, and I can't see how they're going to help much."

"Visual aids are very important to the lesson," Larry responded. "Quality visuals grab the kids' attention, help them to understand the lesson, and cause them to remember it. I never teach without them."

"But these aren't quality," Tim argued. He bit his lip as he struggled to slip a retaining clip into place.

"Okay, so who says you have to use the visuals that came in the lesson packet?"

"So what should I do?"

Larry thought for a moment. "I have a flannelgraph series on the life of Moses," he answered. "I'll loan you the lesson on the Passover. You could visualize the part about the lamb's blood with a fleece, a bowl of ketchup, and an oleander branch."

Tim wrinkled his nose and turned to face Larry. "You mean actually smear some of it around the door frame?"

Larry laughed. "Good guess. Hey, it'll clean up nicely. And your kids will really remember it."

Tim shrugged. "Okay."

"I'll help you make some transparencies for the overhead projector showing the relationship between the Passover and the cross, and we could do some Scripture verse transparencies the same way."

"We don't have a projector. The only equipment in our classroom is a chalkboard, an old piano, a flannel board and an easel with a broken leg."

Larry grimaced. "Doesn't the church have an overhead?"

Tim shrugged. "I don't know. I've never seen anyone using it if we do."

"Why don't you call your pastor tonight and ask? If the church doesn't have one, or you can't have access to it during Children's Church, we'll make the visuals on a poster board chart. Then we'll do the plan of salvation on flashcards with each point of the Romans road on the front of a card and the Scripture verses on the back."

Tim frowned. "All that for just one message?"

Larry used a torque wrench to tighten a large mount bolt. "The visuals are effective, Tim. Once you learn to use them, you'll never want to teach any other way."

"It just seems like an awful lot of work."

"That's probably why some teachers don't use them. But some of the visuals, like the transparencies and flashcards, you can file away and use in other messages. After you've been teaching for awhile it gets easier, 'cause you'll have a whole collection of materials to draw from."

Tim thought it over. "Sounds good to me," he finally said. "That part about the ketchup will really get the kids' attention!"

Visuals are effective. Talk with any teacher who knows his stuff, and he'll tell you just what Larry told Tim: never teach without them.

Visuals enhance your teaching and greatly increase your effectiveness in three main ways: they grab the **attention** of the student; they help him to **understand**

Visual Aids:

1. Grab the *attention* of the students.
2. Help them to *understand* the lesson.
3. Cause them to *remember* it.

26

the lesson; and they cause him to **remember** it. Wow! Talk about effective! What more could you ask for!

Let's look first of all at the power of visuals to gain and hold attention. Your visuals would be worth their weight in gold if they served no other purpose. Basically, there are three types of attention, and a knowledgeable teacher should be familiar with all three.

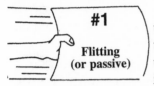

Flitting or passive. This first type of attention requires no effort on the part of the listener. Whatever provides the strongest stimulus to the senses claims the attention of the person in question. When a stronger or more appealing stimulus comes along, the focus is quickly shifted to the new attraction. This type of attention tends to jump rapidly from one object to the next, and is usually the type of attention you can expect from small children.

Let's illustrate **passive attention** this way. Imagine yourself at a bus stop on a dreary Monday morning. You're dragging from a lack of sleep due to spending too much time at a friend's house after church last night. You sit waiting for the bus, half asleep, wishing you had punched out that arrogant alarm clock and gone back to sleep.

A young blond girl in a bright red Camaro comes screeching around the corner, overshoots her turn, and slams the right rear tire against the curb. Downshifting, she recovers and zooms down the street with a roar of exhaust.

"Why do they let these teens drive?" you mutter.

An excited yelp catches your attention, and you turn your head to watch a skinny black poodle chase a calico cat across a well-manicured lawn and up a mulberry tree. The dog circles the tree, barking in aggravation at the cat who hisses in defiance from the safety of a sturdy branch. The dog wanders off, and you go back to fretting about the sales report your boss is sure to ask for.

A hollow metallic clatter startles you, and you look up to see a red-haired boy pedaling erratically down the street, kicking over trash cans along the curb. As he disappears from view, you turn and scan the other direction, hoping for a glimpse of the bus.

While you sit waiting for the bus, your mind is basically in neutral.

Your attention is not focused on any one thing and tends to wander from one stimulus to another.

That's known as **passive attention**. It requires no effort on the part of the listener and responds to a variety of different stimuli. The attention wanders easily, and the strongest stimulus wins.

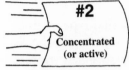

Concentrated or active. This type of attention requires concentration and effort on the part of the listener and is sometimes difficult to maintain for an extended period of time.

Remember when you were in college? You had British literature last period of the day. The class was right after lunch, and you could barely keep your eyes open. You had no interest whatever in the subject matter of that dreary class, but it was required to get your degree, so what did you do? You sat in class day after day, totally bored and disinterested, but forcing yourself to pay attention and absorb enough information to pass the course. That's known as **concentrated attention**, sometimes called **active attention**.

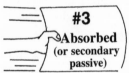

Absorbed or secondary passive. This type of attention requires no effort or concentration on the part of the listener, but it is so strong that other stimuli competing for the attention simply don't have a chance. Let's illustrate.

It's nearly midnight. You're curled up on the couch, watching a spooky movie, waiting for your husband to come home from work. Eerie music sets your nerves on edge as the moon darts behind a cloud, casting a dark, forbidding shadow across the graveyard. A dog howls mournfully in the distance, making your heart beat faster. Your breath comes in short, shallow gasps. Your watchful eyes catch a flicker of movement behind one of the tombstones, and you lean forward.

Suddenly a cold, clammy hand grabs your neck, and a scream of terror escapes your trembling lips. Adrenaline surges through your body as you struggle frantically to free yourself from the deadly grip of the bloodthirsty villain.

A familiar laugh breaks through that split-second of horror, and you turn to see the grinning face of your husband. Relief floods you, and you almost burst into tears.

"Honey, what were you watching?" your husband chuckles. "All I did was touch you, and you nearly jumped through the ceiling!"

Your husband has just witnessed the effects of **absorbed attention**.

What happened? The movie producer used a combination of spooky music, scary sound effects, precise lighting, certain visual stimuli, and the power of your own imagination to place you right in that graveyard with a treacherous murderer. Your heart raced, your pulse quickened, your respiration became labored, and your subconscious called for an order of adrenaline. Your body actually prepared for action, as if you were really facing a life-threatening emergency!

To put it mildly, they had your attention.

Now look back over the three types of attention: **flitting, concentrated,** and **absorbed**. Which would be the ideal for your teaching situation?

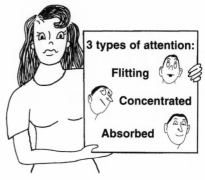

Obviously, the answer is the third type: absorbed.

Very few teachers have the ability to reach the level of absorbed attention from a group of children without the use of visual aids; but the average teacher, with the proper visuals, can expect to gain that level of attention during the lesson! If you want the attention of your students as you teach, if you want to eliminate the discipline problems that arise from disinterest and inattention, if you really want to reach your students' hearts, use visuals!

I like it when my teacher teaches with pictures!

Visual aids, properly used, gain and hold the attention of your students, eliminating many discipline problems in the process!

A second benefit of using visuals to teach is this: they help your students to understand your lessons.

Due to technical difficulties the following program will be presented with the audio alone.

A lot of Bible culture is foreign and unfamiliar

to our modern Western way of life. Your students may struggle just to follow you through a simple Bible story if you are not teaching with visual aids. Sometimes you may not even be aware of the fact that a difficulty exists in the child's mind.

Suppose you are teaching the story of the four men who lowered their palsied friend through the roof to see Jesus, as found in Mark 2. You're zipping merrily along through the story, never realizing that your students are picturing a house with a peaked roof, rather than a Palestinian home with a flat, level roof and stairs rendering access to it. As you tell the story, some of your kids are wondering how four men could carry a man up a ladder! Others are worrying about his rolling off the roof once they get him up there! Visuals could immediately clarify the situation.

Suppose that your lesson involves a scroll, a book foreign to children of today. Why spend several minutes trying to describe it, when you could make one from dowel rods and wallpaper in a matter of minutes! This simple visual would not only create understanding; it would also help hold attention.

Consider also that much of the message of the Bible deals with abstract terms and concepts, while children think in the concrete. They live in a "touch-and-feel" world. How much easier for them to grasp and understand your message if you visualize it as simply as possible.

Are you presenting the plan of salvation? Why not visualize it! Your students will understand far more

> VISUAL AIDS cause the student to REMEMBER the lesson.

readily if they can see and hear your message.

A third benefit of visuals: they cause your students to REMEMBER your lesson!

Communication experts often tell us that we remember **ten percent** of what we **hear** (at least long enough for it to make a change or for us to use the information). Think it through: you prepare and teach a twenty-minute lesson, and your students get only two minutes' worth! Rather discouraging, isn't it?

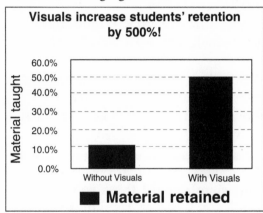

The same experts tell us that we remember as much as **fifty percent** of what we **see** and **hear**. What does that mean to a teacher? Just this: by using visual aids when we teach, we actually multiply our students' retention of the message five times over! That's a five hundred percent (500%) increase!

Those experts also tell us that thirteen percent (13%) of our present knowledge came through the sense of hearing, but seventy-five percent (75%) came through the sense of sight!

What's the most effective way to present the message of the Gospel? Appeal to the sense that facilitates learning most efficiently, the sense of sight.

The world believes in the power of visuals. Hollywood's writers, directors and technicians combine years of expertise with millions of dollars of equipment to present the Devil's message in a powerful, life-changing way. Why should we do less than our best?

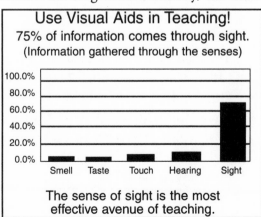

Tim looked up as Larry stepped back into the den. "Okay, so we've got the ketchup, the oleander branch, the fleece and the mixing bowl. I've got your flannelgraph figures and board. The poster board chart looks great, and Lisa should be finished with the plan of salvation flashcards tomorrow.

"But why are we using all this different stuff? It looks like some of these same ideas are in the flannelgraph materials. So why don't we just use those?"

"The key to using visual aids effectively is to use variety," Larry answered. "Visuals don't have to be elaborate to be effective. They can be quite simple. But there should be variety. The best visual in the world gets old if we use it week after week after week.

"I wanted you to get the feel of several different types of visuals. Maybe I'm overdoing it a bit to have this much variety your first time, but the visuals are pretty simple, and I think you'll do well. With this much variety, I think you'll be surprised how well your kids listen."

Tim grinned self-consciously. "I sure hope so."

"You've prayed for that, haven't you?" Larry admonished. "And you've done your part in preparing to the best of your ability. Now let's believe God for the rest." He studied the poster board visual. "Now there's just one more thing."

Tim looked at him questioningly. "What's that?"

"Practice!" his mentor replied. "Practice that lesson out loud, so you can hear how it's going to come out."

Tim laughed. "You're kidding!"

Larry shook his head. "I'm dead serious. Take all your visuals out to the garage tomorrow morning and present your lesson to that cute little Lexus."

Tim looked skeptical.

"No, really!" Larry insisted. "Set up all your visuals in the order that you'll use them day after tomorrow in Children's Church. Then preach the entire message, using the visuals just as you will in class. Don't be discouraged if it doesn't flow smoothly or if you forget some things. That's natural, and that's why you're practicing first. If you take the time to run through your message two or three times, you'll be amazed at how smoothly it will go when you're actually in front of the kids."

Tim shrugged. "I'll give it a try," he replied. "I want to do my very best."

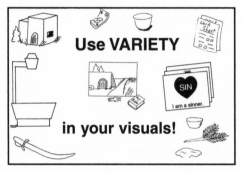

Using Visual Aids Effectively

Let's take a quick look at some simple, practical visuals and the ways to use them most effectively with groups of children.

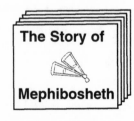

FLASHCARDS—Flashcards are perhaps the simplest of all visual aids in that they are extremely portable, easy to use, require no advance setup, and are easily stored. They can readily be used out-of-doors or in a moving vehicle, and they enable the speaker to move about as they are used in the presentation.

This easy-to-use visual may consist of a set of colorful pictures depicting a Bible story or a modern-day story, or they simply may be key words or phrases printed on cards. A flashcard may be a simple diagram or chart or perhaps a Scripture verse. I've seen flashcards with beautiful artwork, and I've seen others with mere stick figures.

Flashcards come in all sizes. There are tiny, 2" x 3" cards (for use in witnessing to individuals or tiny groups), and there are flashcards as big as a full sheet of poster board!

Here are some basic rules to follow when using this simple but effective visual:

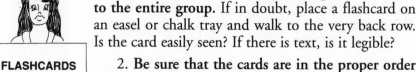

1. **Be sure the card is large enough to be visible to the entire group.** If in doubt, place a flashcard on an easel or chalk tray and walk to the very back row. Is the card easily seen? If there is text, is it legible?

2. **Be sure that the cards are in the proper order before your presentation.** There's hardly anything more embarrassing than finding out right in the middle of the lesson that some of the cards are missing or that the order is jumbled.

Place the cards face up and quickly flip through them, being certain that the first card is on top and the last card is on the bottom.

As you teach the lesson, display the first flashcard. When you are through with it, simply lift it and place it behind the rest of the stack, revealing the next card.

3. **Hold the cards high enough for all to see.** Most teachers have to make a conscious effort to hold the flashcards high enough, especially for a large group.

Be alert as you teach. If you see students in the back stretching to try to see, hold your cards higher.

4. **Pan each card slowly from side to side as you introduce it.** Make sure that those who sit on the extreme edges of the group can see. How many times these kids are left out! Be sure to pass the card across at least two times, and three is better. Remember, flashcards afford you excellent mobility, so walk about as you use them. If you dwell on one card for an extended period of time, remember to pan it slowly across from time to time.

5. **Hold the flashcards steady.** Don't jerk them about. As you teach,

hold the cards in one hand and use the other when you gesture. How distracting and annoying it can be when an animated teacher holds the flashcards in both hands and transfers her gestures through the cards!

6. **Use them in combination with other visuals.** While flashcards may be used to visualize the entire lesson, remember that the key to using visuals effectively is to use variety. Enhance the effectiveness of your flashcards by using them in combination in a lesson with flannelgraph, objects, the overhead projector, etc.

7. **Enlarge them on the opaque projector.** If you have a large group, remember that the opaque projector will project flat, opaque objects in full color—perfect for use with flashcards! Do you have some flashcards that are just too small? Use them to present your lesson with the opaque projector and make them huge!

USING FLASHCARDS

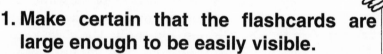

1. Make certain that the flashcards are large enough to be easily visible.
2. Be sure the cards are in the proper order.
3. Hold the cards high enough for all to see.
4. Pan each card slowly from side to side.
5. Hold the cards steady.
6. Use flashcards in combination with other visuals.
7. Use flashcards on the opaque projector.

OBJECTS—Usually the simplest visuals turn out to be the most effective, and this is certainly true of using objects as visual aids.

I often introduce a message on missions by displaying a ten-foot python skin that my parents brought back from Nigeria. When the skin rolls out to its full length across the platform, eyes grow wide with fascination, and a hush falls over the crowd. The fascinating story of how the snake was caught captivates the audience completely, and attention is at its keenest as I lead into the message. Simple, but so effective!

A fellow teacher once shared an interesting story on temptation involving a little mouse named Willie who simply could not resist the tantalizing aroma of a piece of cheese. As a result, he lost his life in a trap. The story was visualized with three flashcards.

As I was practicing the story, an inspiration hit. I replaced the flashcards with a cute little stuffed mouse and a real-life rat trap! That story, used as an introduction to the story of Achan, keeps the kids on the edge of their seats!

GOOD

BETTER

Are you planning to teach the story of David and Goliath? Why not make a sling for David out of a couple of shoelaces and a three-inch

piece of inner tube? (If you plan to try the sling in class, use paper wads rather than rocks!)

The next time you teach the story of Calvary, touch the very souls of your children with the sufferings of Jesus by visualizing with a home-made crown of thorns, whip, hammer and spikes. These simple objects

will greatly increase the impact of your other lesson visuals such as flash-cards, overhead transparencies or flannelgraph.

 The lesson on the feeding of the five thousand can be brought to life with the aid of five dinner rolls and two frozen fish fillets.

Milk, candles, shoes, bread, hammers, water, garden tools, flashlights, coins, computer diskettes, books, maps, hats, apples and keys— what do these items have in common? Simple as they are, any of them can be used as visual aids to enhance a Bible lesson!

Are you planning to share a story about a man who was lost? Why not display a road map as you tell the story? Do you have a gripping · illustration about a child who steals from her mother's purse? Why not use a woman's purse and three or four dollar bills as visuals?

Think through every Bible story or modern-day illustration that you use and find some way to enhance it with objects, even if the story is already visualized in another form. The objects, when added to the other visuals, make the presentation even more appealing and attention-catching.

Appeal to the natural curiosity of your students by concealing an object in a box or paper sack, then bringing it to class. Introduce your lesson by referring to the object in the sack, talking about its importance in our lives, its value or rarity, etc., without revealing what the object is.

When curiosity is at its peak, draw the object from the sack and use it to lead into the lesson.

A pastor in a large church in Phoenix once used this method to very good advantage in a Sunday evening service.

Displaying a large wooden box on the platform, he informed his audience that it contained the most powerful weapon in the world. For five minutes he kept the congregation in suspense as he compared it to nuclear weaponry, chemical warfare, etc. He told how this weapon could be used to destroy nations, families, individuals and churches. When the congregation was completely captivated, he reached into the box and pulled out a four-pound beef tongue, then preached a message on James 3!

This was a crude form of visualization to be sure, but twenty years later, I still remember the message!

Everyday objects can become valuable visual aids. They are easy to use, portable, and add tremendous variety to your other visuals.

OVERHEAD PROJECTOR—Here's a visual aid that is extremely versatile. It can be used to project Scripture verses, maps, charts, Bible stories and lesson applications. Ready-made transparencies may be used, the speaker may write or sketch during the presentation, or a combination of methods may be employed. Transparencies range from the traditional black-on-clear to dazzling full color. This machine can even be used to visualize Bible stories in silhouette shadows with small cardboard cut-outs!

THE
OVERHEAD
PROJECTOR
CAN BE FUN
TO USE!

The overhead projector can be used effectively with almost any size group. I've seen projectors used with small classes of five or six kids, and I once watched a lecturer use one with a crowd of three thousand! With a giant screen and a super-bright overhead, his visuals were clearly visible from the back of the huge auditorium.

The teacher with an overhead actually has push-button control of the listeners' attention. When he switches the machine on, every eye automatically darts to the brightly-lit screen. When he switches it off, all eyes automatically jump back to the speaker. What power!

I personally prefer the 3M projectors over the other makes on the market. The 3M machines are well designed and moderately priced. You'll find other brands priced slightly lower than the 3M, but in my opinion you won't be happy with them.

The 3M Company also makes quality transparency films in a variety of colors, and they give tremendous service to the customer. I once made five hundred transparencies at one time with 3M film, but used the wrong type film for that particular copier. 3M replaced the entire order of film, gave me an extra hundred sheets, and charged me only for the shipping!

Again, you may find cheaper films on the market, but the consistent quality of the 3M products make them well worth the price. To locate a 3M dealer near you, call:

1-800-328-1371

The three components that you need to consider when using the overhead are: the screen, the overhead projector and the transparencies that you will project as you teach the lesson.

The screen. It's possible to project your visuals on a light-colored wall, of course, but it is usually preferable to use a screen. Projection screens come in three different surfaces: matte white, silver and glass beaded. The best surface by far for use with the overhead is matte white.

Many tripod-type screens come with a keystone eliminator, a hanger-like device at the top that allows the top of the screen to be angled forward a few inches. This eliminates "keystoning" (that odd, upside-down trapezoid shape you sometimes see on the screen) and allows the projected image to be rectangular.

If you are planning to use a wall-mounted or ceiling-mounted screen, mount it six or eight inches from the wall so that the bottom may be pulled back against the wall, again eliminating the "keystoning" effect.

The screen should not be positioned in the center of the room, parallel to the wall, as one would suppose. The speaker blocks the view of much of the audience if this is the case. Rather, position or mount the screen to one side at an angle (to your right if you are right-handed, to your left if you are left-handed). This actually allows your students a clearer view of the screen.

The projector. Long before class starts, position your projector on a small, sturdy table or projection stand. (Be sure that it is very stable. An undisciplined three-year-old once sent my projector crashing to the floor.) Turn the projector on and focus it properly on the screen, moving your table gently to the point where the image fills the screen in a neat rectangle. (Be very cautious about moving the projector while it is on; this can blow the bulb.)

Once the projector is properly focused, unplug it and move the cord so that no one trips over it on the way to his seat.

When using ready-made transparencies, place them in a neat stack beside the machine. Carefully flip through them to ascertain that they are in the order in which they will be used.

As you present your message, place the first transparency on the stage of the projector, then switch the projector on. Each time you change a transparency, switch the machine off, change transparencies, then switch it back on. This saves your audience from staring at a glaring white screen and eliminates the distraction of seeing the old image slide out of focus to be replaced by the newer one. (Don't worry about the bulb; it was designed for this type of usage. I use my projector five nights a week and average two or three years per bulb.)

An easy way to make certain that your transparencies are perfectly aligned on the screen is to use Faith Venture Visual's Insta-Frame. This handy device consists of a plastic frame around a piece of tempered glass. Once the Insta-Frame is in position on the projector, your teaching transparencies may be placed in it, and they are automatically aligned perfectly on the screen! There's no need to turn and check the screen. I never use my overhead without my Insta-Frame.

The Insta-Frame may be ordered from:
Creative Training Techniques
7620 West 78th Street
Minneapolis, MN 55439
1–800–383–9210

42

The transparencies. There are several publishing houses that produce lesson transparencies, but quite often it's preferable to make your own. Transparencies may be made on the plain paper copier using special transparency film available at any office supply retailer. These films are available in clear, red, yellow, green and blue. Computer-generated transparencies may be printed out on an inkjet or laser printer, and the films are available in a variety of colors. Color printers are capable of producing beautiful, full-color transparencies!

Your local quick-service print shop will usually make transparencies for you at a reasonable cost. Some of the high-tech, ultra-modern print shops can make full-color transparencies from color posters or flashcards. These can cost as much as three dollars per transparency, but it can be worth it if you will use the transparencies a number of times. You'll usually need a letter of permission from the publisher who holds the copyright on the original.

Bible story coloring books, flashcard sets, clip art books, computer graphics, illustrated Bible story books, posters and even flannelgraph figures can be sources of artwork for your transparencies. If you have any artistic ability at all, simple sketches and even "stick figures" can be used to illustrate your message. Your computer also can be used to produce professional-quality text or captions for your work.

Here are some basic rules for making transparencies:

1. **Use a horizontal format.** On the computer, this is known as "landscape" as opposed to "portrait." Horizontal transparencies actually have more usable space than vertical, and the resulting image fits the shape of the screen better.

2. **Keep the transparency simple.** Don't clutter it with numerous graphics and lots of text. It's best to present one basic idea with each transparency.

3. **Keep text to a minimum, and make it large.** When visualizing Scripture verses, place one verse per transparency—two at most. Your lettering should be at least 3/8" high (27 point), and larger if possible. Many times teachers try to type their transparency masters. The result is that the lettering is far too small and is almost impossible to read on the screen.

4. **Use a variety of colors.** When planning a lesson that will utilize

several transparencies, use several different colors of film for a little variety in the presentation.

5. **Use transparency frames.** These help protect your visuals and are available at any office supply store. If you plan to use the Insta-Frame, you'll have to make your own frames from poster board; the ready-made ones simply won't fit.

To make a transparency frame, cut an 8½" x 11" rectangle from a sheet of poster board (you'll get six of these from a full 22" x 28" sheet). Using a straight edge and razor blade or Exacto knife, cut out the center of the rectangle, leaving a ¾" wide frame. (I usually cut the first one precisely, then use it as a template to mark the others for cutting.)

Using the straight edge and Exacto knife, cut your transparency down to 8" x 10½". Now center it on the frame and tape it in place with half-inch cellophane tape.

For maximum protection of your valuable transparencies, tape a clear 8" x 10½" sheet of acetate (write-on film) to the frame, then tape your transparency over that, followed by another sheet of acetate. Your transparency is now sandwiched between two clear sheets and is protected from scratches.

6. **File your transparencies for future use.** Your local print shop will usually sell you 8½" x 11" boxes at a nominal cost, and they provide excellent storage for your transparencies.

MAKING TRANSPARENCIES

Use a horizontal format.
Keep the transparency simple.
Keep text to a minimum.
Make it large.
Use a variety of colors.
Use transparency frames.
File your transparencies for future use.

FLANNELGRAPH—Mention the term "visual aids," and most people immediately think of flannelgraph. This teaching medium has

certainly been overused by some, but it is still very effective when used correctly and when used with other forms of visuals.

Colorful background scenes add to the beauty of this visual, but they are not absolutely necessary. Flannelgraph lessons are very effective when used on a plain flannel board with no background scene.

If you do use background scenes, consider this technique for ease and proficiency when changing scenes. Obtain large sheets of corrugated cardboard from your local furniture dealer (assure him that it is a recycling project) and cut them into 27" x 36" rectangles. Lay a scene out on a sheet of cardboard, staple it taut along the edges, then trim the board out with silver duct tape.

Place your scenes on the easel in the order in which you will use them. As you teach the lesson, you can now change scenes without having to remove the figures or overlays!

Much has been written about the proper use of flannelgraph, so we will limit this discussion to a few simple rules:

1. **Make certain that your flannel board is visible to all.** If your easel is not tall enough, add new bolts and move the support tray higher, or add extensions to the legs. Discipline problems often arise when a child stands up to see, thus blocking the view of those behind him. Get that flannel board up high!

Then make sure that your students at the extreme outside edges of the group can see the board. Sit in the last chair on each side on the front row to check, and adjust the board as necessary.

2. **Practice placing the figures on the board.** With a little practice, you'll be sure to place the figures at the right place so that the perspective is right. Remember, as you move a figure up on the board, it appears to grow larger, and as you move it down, it shrinks. How many times I've seen teachers slap their figures on the flannel board in such a haphazard manner that one person appears to be four feet tall while another is ten feet tall! During your lesson preparation time, get the proper perspective by placing the figures on the board, then stepping back and checking the effect. Of course, you want those figures on straight, so practice, practice, practice!

3. **Double check that your flannelgraph figures are in the proper order before you begin.** Your lesson loses its "flow" when you have to stop and hunt for the next figure.

4. **Don't turn your back to place your figures.** Learn to position your flannel figures on your board without turning your back to your audience. Unless you are wearing a wireless mike, your voice fades every time you turn.

5. **Don't have your figures serve "double duty."** A figure that is used one week to represent a negative character such as Judas Iscariot should not be used the next Sunday to represent a positive, godly character. This creates confusion in the minds of your students.

6. **Don't overuse this visual aid.** Flannelgraph can be a very effective visual aid, but it loses much of its effectiveness when used time after time. Your students enjoy variety! Use the flannel board in combination with other types of visuals. Skip the flannel board entirely on occasion. If there is one visual that has seen too much use, it would be the flannel board.

USING FLANNELGRAPH
1. Make sure the flannel board is visible to all.
2. Practice positioning the figures.
3. Double check—figures in proper order?
4. Don't turn your back to place the figures.
5. Don't have your figures serve double-duty.
6. Don't overuse flannelgraph!

DRY ERASE BOARDS—This is a simple visual aid that is inexpensive, easy to use, and brings variety to your presentations. The board can be wall-mounted or used on an easel; the smaller versions can be handheld. Markers are available at any teaching supply or office supply store.

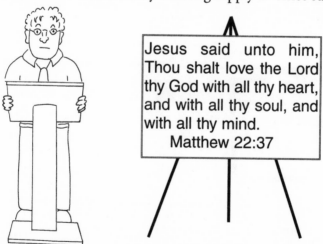

Jesus said unto him, Thou shalt love the Lord thy God with all thy heart, and with all thy soul, and with all thy mind.
Matthew 22:37

Ready-made marker boards are readily available, but it is much more economical to make your own. Simply buy a 4' x 8' sheet of Marlite (white board) at your local hardware or building supply store.

Wall-mount a 4' x 4' or 4' x 6' section, then trim it out with an aluminum or wood frame. If you plan to use a marker board on an easel, simply cut the sheet into 27" x 36" sheets, then trim the edges out with duct tape. To make a double-duty visual board, spread white glue across the back surface of the board (use a piece of cardboard to "squee-gee" it thinly and evenly across the surface), then stretch a sheet of solid-color flannel

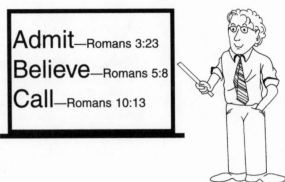

across it. Trim the excess material around the edges, then trim the board out with duct tape. You now have a flannel board on one side and a dry erase board on the other!

Cut the leftover pieces of white board into 12" x 16" "walkie-talkie" boards and trim them out with duct tape. The "walkie-talkie" board may be carried about as you teach. Use it to write down key words or phrases, draw simple diagrams, etc.

Be sure to store your dry erase markers tightly capped and horizontal. They dry out if left standing on end.

Pictures and videos and sand tables and sketch boards and flip charts and posters and models and puppets and filmstrips and costumes and handouts—there are so many other visuals to try! Learn to use them all, and bring tremendous variety to your teaching situation. Your class will sparkle with new life and enthusiasm, and your students will learn and grow.

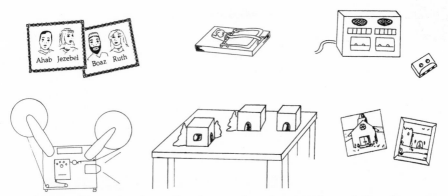

Remember, visuals grab the students' **attention**, help them to **understand** the lesson, and cause them to **remember** it. Your effectiveness as a teacher is greatly enhanced every time you use these dynamic teaching tools!

"Once you see how effective your teaching becomes when you use visuals, you'll never teach again without them," Larry told Tim. "Visuals help immensely!"

Tim nodded. "I believe you."

Debbie Edwards slipped into the den and handed Tim a couple of two-liter bottles of Coke Classic.

"What are these for?" Tim asked.

"Use them as behavior awards," Larry answered. "Just open Children's Church with the announcement that your workers are watching for the quietest boy and the quietest girl. Display the Cokes and tell the kids that the winners take them home. You'll be delighted at the response! If the kids forget and start getting restless at any point, simply mention the contest, or even just pick up one of the bottles. The kids will instantly shape up.

"Next week I'll show you some of the behavior-award games we use, but I think you have enough to remember right now.

We'll use the Cokes for simplicity."

Tim headed for the door, clutching the various visual aids. "Thanks for all your help, Brother. I'm excited about this! I can't wait till Sunday morning!"

So, to be effective, you must...

Prepare.
Use visuals.

Perry Pedagogue

I really don't have time to prepare visuals for class.

To be honest, I really don't think visuals are all that important!

But, I do wish that my students would listen better!

How many different VISUAL AIDS have you used?

___ Flashcards	___ Sand Table
___ Objects	___ Blacklight Scene
___ Charts & Graphs	___ Sketch Board
___ Maps	___ Flip Charts
___ Flannelgraph	___ Posters
___ Overhead Projector	___ Bulletin Boards
___ Chalkboard	___ Pictures
___ Marker Board	___ Models
___ Video	___ Puppets
___ Movie Projector	___ Role-Play
___ Filmstrip Projector	___ Costumes
___ Slide Projector	___ Handouts

Check the list for any visuals that you have never used, then learn to use them to enhance your teaching ministry!

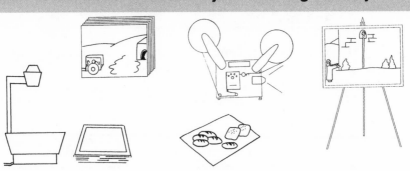

Evaluating My Use of Visual Aids

YES   NO

___ ___   1. Do I use a variety of visual aids?

___ ___   2. Are my visuals neat and attractive?

___ ___   3. Do they call attention to the lesson rather than to themselves?

___ ___   4. Are my visuals large enough to be clearly seen by every student?

___ ___   5. Do I place flannel boards, etc., high enough for all to see?

___ ___   6. Do I prepare early enough in the week so that I have time to gather the necessary teaching materials?

___ ___   7. Do I make sure that all visuals are in the proper order or sequence before class starts?

___ ___   8. Do I have my visuals so well organized that the program flows smoothly?

___ ___   9. Do my visuals help hold the attention of my students?

___ ___ 10. Are my teaching materials set up and ready before the first student arrives?

___ ___ 11. Do I fully understand the reasons for using visual aids?

___ ___ 12. Do I enjoy preparing and using visual aids?

Ask Andy!

Dear Andy,

    I recently saw an expert communicator use an overhead projector at a training seminar, and it made for a really sharp presentation. My question is this—how do I choose the right projector for my class?

Jerry Attrix

Dear Jerry,

    There are a lot of different overhead projectors to choose from, but you want to buy the right machine the first time. Here's what I would look for:

    1. Brightness. Buy a projector that puts out 2500 to 2700 lumens. (A lot of projectors are in the 1500 to 1600 range, but you want a brighter projector than this.) The brighter the light, the better your transparencies look on the screen.

    2. Cooling fan on the side. Don't buy a projector with the fan on the front (facing the audience). This can be a major distraction to your students. Make sure that the fan is whisper quiet.

    3. Power switch on top. I've seen a number of overheads with the power switch down on the back side, which forces you to fumble for it every time you turn the machine on. Get a projector that has the switch on top, allowing you easy access to it.

    4. Bulb changer. Many of today's projectors have a spare projection bulb inside the machine. If you blow

the first bulb during your presentation, you simply flip a switch to slide the spare into place. Smooth!

5. Fold-down projector head. This convenience is designed for those who travel with their projector, as I do.

Hope this helps!

Andy

Dear Andy,

When I use a cover sheet on my overhead, it always falls off when I get toward the bottom of the transparency. Any suggestions?

Paige Turner

Dear Paige,

Here's a simple solution. Use a stiff material for your cover sheet (such as card stock or poster board). Tape two or three nickels to the top corner. The weight of the coins will keep your cover sheet in place, even when you reach the bottom of the transparency and the sheet extends beyond the edge of the transparency and beyond the edge of the projector.

Good luck with your cover-ups!

Andy

Dear Andy,

I love to use flannelgraph, but every time I do, the kids in the back rows stand up to see better. This, of course, causes problems for the kids behind them, and we end up with fights in class.

How can I get my students to stay in their seats, rather than standing up? It's become a major problem.

Kay Oss

Dear Kay,

As I see it, the problem is simply the fact that your visuals are not high enough! You need to raise your flannel board.

This can be done in one of two ways: drill new holes and raise the tray that holds the board, or extend the length of the legs. Get that flannel board up high!

Yours is a common problem. You would not believe how many short easels I have seen in Sunday school classrooms.

Andy

3.

BALLOON BUST BOARDS AND OTHER BENEFICIAL BEHAVIOR BOONS

Monday morning Tim Wellington hurried into the work area to find his friend Larry Edwards laying out his tools on the workbench. Larry looked up as he entered. "Good morning, Tim. How did Children's Church go?"

"Fantastic!" Tim replied as he punched a fist into the air to show his delight. "There was such a difference from last week! It was almost hard to believe it was the same group of kids. They weren't perfect, of course, and there were still problems; but if they improve as much next Sunday as they did yesterday, they'll be little angels!"

Larry laughed. "I wouldn't expect that if I were you," he said. "But the preparation paid off, didn't it?"

"I'll say it did!" Tim agreed. "It was unbelievable! The kids actually listened during the lesson. Lisa and I are already working on next week's lesson and program."

Larry smiled. "How'd the Bible game go?"

"Super! The kids really went for it. I was surprised at how well they answered the questions. You know one thing that really helped? The Cokes! When I told them about the contest, the kids immediately sat so still and quiet you would have thought they were wax figures! I wouldn't have believed that those kids could get that quiet."

Larry adjusted the strap on a new pair of safety glasses, then tried them on. "Behavior awards help tremendously," he agreed. "It's amazing how much motivation they provide."

"We're gonna use the Cokes every Sunday," Tim declared. "Lisa and I both decided they were worth the investment."

Larry shook his head. "You can't use them every week."

Tim frowned and looked up from the parts bin. "Why not?"

"They would lose their effectiveness after just a few weeks," Larry explained. "Just as with the other parts of your program, your behavior-award contest needs variety. When a teacher uses the same behavior award week after week, the kids lose interest, and the incentive is gone. Keep it new and fresh and exciting."

"What would you suggest?"

"I'll help you make a Balloon Bust Board," Larry offered. "I've got some sheathing material left over from the addition we did on the house. We can paint it white, and Debbie will trim it out for you with a bulletin board border. All you have to get are the darts, balloons and prizes."

"How does it work?"

"Staple fifteen or twenty balloons to the board. Each balloon will have a slip of paper inside naming a prize—Cokes, squirt guns, candy bars, stuff like that. Just have the winning kids come up to the balloon board three or four minutes before dismissal. Give them each several throws. Each time they pop a balloon, they win the prize named on the slip of paper."

Tim nodded. "Sounds like fun."

"You can use it for three or four weeks, then move on to something else before the kids have a chance to get tired of it."

"Your middle name should have been *Variety*."

Larry laughed. "Variety keeps things fresh and new, and it keeps the kids excited about learning," he answered. "And that's when your discipline problems are at a minimum."

Behavior awards are effective. Used properly, these powerful tools can motivate your students to unusually good behavior in class, making your job as a teacher so much easier! Why teach a rowdy, disruptive class when you could easily be teaching a quiet, attentive class? Behavior awards can make the difference.

As a teacher in today's Sunday school, Children's Church or Wednesday night club program, you are dealing with a generation of kids who are undisciplined, disrespectful and unruly; yet your hands are tied. You can't spank these little brats! You can't stand them in the corner or assign them extra homework. So what are you to do?

Approach discipline problems from the positive side! Work overtime to develop the most interesting, exciting and challenging teaching hour that your kids have ever seen. Then make your job of teaching even easier by introducing behavior-award contests.

Your students will start working to win the contest from the moment you announce it. Usually, if you have a well-planned teaching program, they forget the contest and become intrigued by your teaching activities. The behavior contest simply sets the stage for effective learning to take place. Your well-prepared lesson has an even greater impact because of the ideal teaching situation created by the behavior contest.

"My class loves the Balloon Bust Board! It's effective as an incentive to good behavior."

59

USING BEHAVIOR AWARDS EFFECTIVELY

After twenty-five years of using behavior awards with children in Sunday school, Children's Church, public school assemblies, AWANA Clubs, King's Kids, junior camps, backyard Bible clubs and just about every other teaching situation you can imagine, here are some guidelines we have developed:

1. **Announce the behavior contest early in the teaching hour.** After opening with a song and prayer, flag salutes, or whatever, simply announce: "Today we are watching for three quiet students. We will choose a quiet boy, a quiet girl and a third quiet person, who may be a boy or a girl. Those three winners will get to play THE BALLOON BUST BOARD! If you want to be a winner, here's what you need to do…"

2. **Make the award on an individual basis, and base it solely on behavior.** Don't announce that you are looking for the quietest row or the quietest team. Your students will quickly learn that everyone's chances of winning evaporate when one kid on the row messes up. It's always best to keep it on an individual basis. Every student knows that winning or losing is dependent solely on his own behavior.

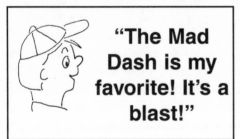

"The Mad Dash is my favorite! It's a blast!"

3. **Keep the rules to a minimum.** Many times teachers make a list of eight or ten or twelve rules for classroom behavior, and the students have a hard time remembering them.

CLASSROOM RULES
1. No talking while the teacher is talking.
2. Keep feet and hands to yourself.
3. Do not throw anything.
4. No rocking on the chairs.
5. Listen to the instructions the first time.
6. Raise your hands before talking.
7. No playing around.
8. Leave other people's things alone.
9. No fighting.
10. Stay in your seats unless you have permission.

(Exactly as copied from a Sunday school classroom wall)

CLASSROOM RULES
1. Sit up straight.
2. No talking.

Instead, simply announce, "If you want to play *The Price Is Right* today, just follow these two rules: 1. Sit up straight; 2. No talking."

These two simple rules cover a multitude of sins! You'll soon find that if your students are following these two rules, everything else falls in line. Keep the rules simple.

4. **Plan the number of winners in proportion to the size of your group.** If you have a class of fifteen or twenty, one or two winners would be sufficient. But if you have a group of sixty or eighty, you'll want to choose five or six winners, with ten or twelve winners on occasion. If you teach a group of two or three hundred, you may want to choose as many as fifteen or twenty winners!

When you have multiple winners with a large group, select three or four as "grand prize winners" to play a behavior-award game such as *Let's Make a Deal* or *The Mad Dash*, then pass out smaller prizes such as Cokes or candy bars to a number of other winners.

5. **Let your workers select the winners.** If you are presenting the Bible message or lesson, your attention needs to be focused on the message rather than choosing winners. Assign this duty in advance so that the students do not know from week to week who is watching.

I like to call these behavior judges "secret agents." Sometimes they are referred to as "hawk-eyes," "super snoopers," or simply "spotters."

If you do not have any other adult workers in your class, the job of spotter, of course, falls to you.

6. **Select winners from the "church kids" as well as the "bus kids."** Many times the children of church members are left out as if they should be expected to behave without any reward. This can be very frustrating to these children. Make sure that *everyone* has an equal chance to win!

If you see one of your "troublemakers" making a special effort to be good, allow him or her to win with less than perfect behavior. Any kid who tries his best for several weeks without winning can become discouraged, and then his behavior becomes even worse than before.

7. **Use behavior-award games rather than simply handing the child a prize.** Your behavior contest will be far more exciting and much more effective if you make a game of presenting the prizes. Rather than simply handing out prizes, allow the winners to play *Swapper Shopper*, *Let's Make a Deal*, or *Crazy Cube*. You'll find that your students will try much harder to win if there is a game involved.

8. **Use variety in your behavior-award games.** Play a behavior-award game such as *Fabulous Fishing* for three weeks or so, then switch to another game such as *The Mad Dash* for two or three weeks. Play *Mystery Toss* one time, then use *Let's Make a Deal* or *Balloon Bust Board* for several weeks. You'll quickly learn which behavior games are the most popular with your group; therefore, use the more successful games more frequently or for longer periods of time.

Always remember that variety keeps interest high, and never use a behavior award so often that the students grow tired of it.

Keep a written record of when each game was used so you'll know when to repeat it.

Behavior awards make your job much easier!

BEHAVIOR-AWARD GAMES

Listed below are several of the most popular and successful behavior awards that we have used in our ministry with kids. You'll soon come up with some ideas of your own!

1. **BALLOON BUST BOARD**—This is a winner with any group of Primaries or Juniors. Insert paper slips naming different prizes into a number of balloons, inflate them, then fasten them to a sheet of sheathing or paneling with tape or thumbtacks. (Cluster the balloons toward the center of the board.)

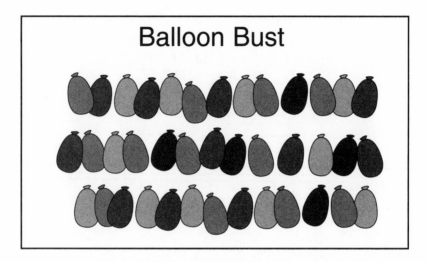

Trim the board with an attractive border, and place a brightly-colored sign reading "Balloon Bust" at the top or center. The board may be placed on an easel or table, propped up on a chalkboard tray, or even fastened to the wall.

The winners throw three or four darts from a short distance, receiving the prizes named in any balloons they pop. Plan for each student to pop at least one or two balloons, and give him additional darts until he succeeds.

(Note: Use extreme caution with this game. Be certain that no spectators, including teachers, are anywhere near the target area. Children can be unbelievably wild with a dart. With a class of younger students, you might even consider taping a dart to the end of an 18" dowel rod and having the winners simply poke the balloons. Not quite as much fun, but a lot safer!)

Be sure to make the slips of paper large enough to find when the balloons pop. I once made the slips so tiny that they were almost impossible to find when they came flying out of the balloons.

If your students are anything like mine, *Balloon Bust* will be a winner!

2. **SWAPPER SHOPPER**—In this behavior-award game, the winners have the opportunity to try again if they are not satisfied with the prize they receive the first time. The child who trades and tries again, however, may end up with a less desirable prize! (This might provide a

"teachable moment" on the importance of being content.)

To prepare *Swapper Shopper,* display nine to twelve prizes on a table. These items should range from small prizes to one or two really desirable items. Write the name of each prize on a separate index card, insert the cards into individual envelopes, and place the envelopes on the table in front of the prizes.

To play the game, select the winners, and then allow each winner to select one envelope. When the child opens the envelope and discovers which prize he has won, he then has the option of keeping it or trying once more by selecting a second envelope and thus receiving a different prize. Caution the students before they make their selections that once they decide to go for the trade, they may **not** trade back, even if the second item is less desirable.

VARIATION: Play *Swapper Shopper* with the prizes concealed in individual paper sacks. When a student opens her sack and discovers her prize, she has the option of keeping or swapping but has no idea what prizes are available.

3. **FABULOUS FISHING**—This game has been used with success for decades at county fairs and carnivals, so it's certainly not original with me. But it's a lot of fun, and I think your students will enjoy it.

Display a number of prizes on a table, each marked with an identifying numeral. (The smaller, less desirable prizes are marked with the lower numbers, the larger ones with higher numbers.) Mark the same

number of four-inch poster board fish with the corresponding numerals, slide a paper clip onto the mouth of each, and drop them into a large paper grocery sack. The behavior contest winners "fish" with a magnet on the end of a two-foot line dangling from a tree-limb "fishing pole."

When a fish is "caught," the numeral on the fish designates which prize the student receives. If a child "catches" more than one fish, allow him to keep the fish with the lowest number. (Explain that "it's the big ones that get away." This will discourage him from purposely trying to catch multiple fish.)

VARIATION: Position one of your workers behind your puppet screen or puppet stage and allow the winning students to "fish" over the top. (The magnet would be replaced with a spring-type clothespin in this case.) As the child fishes, the worker places the child's prize in the jaws of the clothespin, then gives a tiny tug as the signal for the child to pull it up. (A slip-knot loop should be tied in the string for heavy prizes such as a two-liter soda or bag of candy. Tighten the loop around the prize, rather than using the clothespin.)

ANOTHER VARIATION: Prepare six cards with a numeral (1, 2 or 3) on each. Place the cards facedown on a table or lectern before the fishing begins. Allow each winning student to draw a number card which tells him how many fish he is allowed to catch.

4. **CRAZY CUBE**—This idea came from Brother Bill Van Hoesen of

Faith Baptist Church in Godfrey, Illinois, and I share it here with his permission. Thanks, Bill!

Make a four-inch, six-sided cube (is there any other kind?) from cardboard or wood, and number the sides from 1 to 6. Prepare a cardboard screen with two armholes at an appropriate height for your students. Select six different prizes, one of them being larger and more valuable or desirable than the rest.

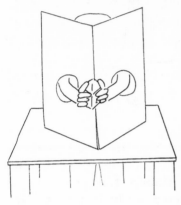

When playing *Crazy Cube* at the end of class time, display the various prizes and tell the class which prize each number wins, pointing out that number 6 is the grand prize.

Each behavior-award winner takes a turn stepping behind the screen, inserting his hands through the holes, and having the *Crazy Cube* placed in his hands. Once the cube is in his possession, he has ten seconds to try to turn it so that the number 6 faces away from him and toward the audience. The contestant cannot see the cube, of course, but the audience may shout directions!

At the end of ten seconds, honk a bicycle horn or ring a bell as a signal to stop. The number facing forward designates the prize the student has won.

5. **LET'S MAKE A DEAL**—This has always been a favorite with every group of children we have ever used it with.

Before your students arrive, place one or more prizes in each of three

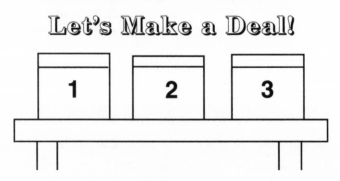

brightly-painted wooden boxes with lids. The numerals 1, 2 and 3 should be stenciled on the front of the boxes. Shoe boxes or decorative lunch sacks with the numerals in Magic Marker work well with smaller groups. Two of the boxes should contain desirable prizes, while the third contains a "whammy" (a diaper, potato, or some other useless item).

As you teach, an unidentified worker ("secret agent") selects three winners from the class. Tell the students that one winner will be chosen from the boys, one from the girls, and the third winner may be either a boy or girl.

During the last two or three minutes of class, play *Let's Make a Deal*. The three winners are each handed a prize, then given the option of keeping it or trading it for one of the boxes, not knowing, of course, what the boxes contain. Caution them in advance about the whammy. (If a child receives the whammy, give him an opportunity to trade back by choosing a number between one and three, etc. If he chooses the wrong number, be ready with a small consolation prize after class.)

Let's Make a Deal has always been a winner with "my kids," and I'm sure that your students will also love it!

6. **MYSTERY TOSS**—This behavior-award game is unusual in that the behavior contest winners attempt to win prizes, not knowing which student will receive them!

After selecting your best-behaved students, write the name of each on the bottom of a large paper grocery sack. Without allowing the contestants to see the names, place the sacks side by side several feet from a tape line on the floor. (The sacks may be placed on the floor, but placing them on a table makes the game more visible to the rest of the class.)

Have the contestants stand behind the tape line. Give each a quantity of wrapped candy (penny candy or fun-size candy bars). They attempt to throw the candy into the sacks, not knowing, of course, which sack belongs to which student! At the conclusion of the game, each student receives the candy in the sack with his or her name.

VARIATION: Give a nice prize to the student with the least candy in his sack. You may choose to announce this before the game begins or keep it secret for a surprise at the conclusion of the game.

ANOTHER VARIATION: Display a number of prizes on a table, each marked with a number. Mark an equal number of Ping-Pong balls with corresponding numerals. Prepare the target sacks as described above. As each ball is tossed, announce which prize it designates. When all the Ping-Pong balls have landed in the sacks, distribute the prizes to the designated winners.

7. **THE MAD DASH**—This behavior-award game generates an unbelievable amount of excitement, both among the participants and spectators. I must admit that, even as a teacher, I enjoy watching my students play *The Mad Dash.*

The Mad Dash

Place a number of prizes on a table with three or four paper grocery sacks ten or twelve feet away on the floor. (Open any bags of fun-size candy bars, ten-packs of gum, six-packs of Coke, etc., and spread the contents around for a greater number of prizes.) At a given signal, three or four selected winners race to the table, grab one item, then race back

68

and drop it in their sacks. Taking only one item at a time, they collect as many prizes as they can in fifteen seconds!

Another form of *The Mad Dash* is to place six or eight simple tasks on the table for the winner to perform in thirty seconds (drinking a cup of water, stacking eight or ten blocks, threading a needle, etc.). Each time the child completes a task, he wins an additional prize. You can't possibly imagine the excitement this behavior game will generate!

8. **BEANBAG TOSS**—Place five small boxes in a row on an eight-foot folding table with as much space between them as possible. Obtain several beanbags (or Ping-Pong balls) for the students to throw. Buy several of each of five different prizes ranging from small, inexpensive items to large, more valuable items. (Example: The five prizes might be, in this order: a ring, a candy bar, a squirt gun, a two-liter soft drink, and a Super Soaker squirt gun.)

Have each contestant stand behind a tape line at the end of the table and attempt to throw the beanbag into the first box to win the first prize. If he is successful, he throws at the second in an attempt to win the second prize, then the third, etc. Once he misses a throw, his turn ends, and he receives the prizes designated by his successful throws.

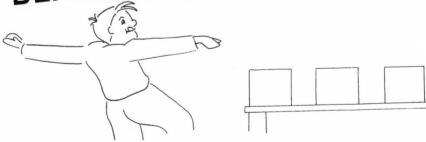

(Hint: Experiment before class to determine how far away the targets should be for the age group of your students. It's best to have the targets at such a distance that almost everyone completes the first and second throw successfully, but very few can make the last.)

VARIATION: Place larger targets such as laundry baskets on chairs at greater distances and have the contestants throw beanbags or tennis balls.

Effective Use of Behavior Awards

1. Announce the behavior contest at the start.
2. Make the awards on an individual basis.
3. Base them solely on behavior.
4. Keep the rules to a minimum.
5. Size of group determines number of winners.
6. Have your assistants select the winners.
7. Include the "church kids."
8. Use behavior-award games.
9. Use a variety of behavior-award games.

The behavior games explained above have all been used successfully with groups of children, but don't get locked in to one or two favorites to the point of overuse! Behavior-award games provide the greatest motivation for good behavior when there is variety. So, use a particular behavior award for just a few weeks, then move on to another, and then another. In a few months, return to the first game, and your students will again respond with enthusiasm.

Ask the Lord to help you to be creative, and design some behavior games of your own!

Behavior-award games are effective!

Wednesday night after church Tim called Larry. "Hey, I've got the balloons and the darts for the *Balloon Bust Board*. And Lisa's gonna pick up a bunch of prizes from Wal-Mart tomorrow."

"Great!" Larry responded. "Why don't you stop by after work Friday, and we'll paint the board?"

"I'll plan on it!" Tim said eagerly. "Hey, here's why I'm calling.

One of the Sunday school teachers just shared a neat idea with Lisa, and I thought I'd pass it on to you. It sounds like a clever way to choose the winners. It's called 'secret seat.'"

"You designate one or more seats ahead of time," Larry interrupted, "and if the kid sitting in the secret seat has been good, he or she gets the behavior award."

"How did you know?" Tim asked.

"That idea has been around for years. Sometimes it's called 'the quiet seat prize.' But it's not effective."

"What do you mean?" Tim asked, a puzzled look on his face. "It sounded like a neat idea! What's wrong with it?"

"Think it through," Larry urged. "Who wins the prize?"

"The best-behaved kid," Tim answered.

"Not really!" Larry replied. "The best-behaved kid wins only if he happens to be sitting in the lucky seat. If not, he wins nothing, no matter how well he behaves. Kids figure that out pretty quickly, and it doesn't provide much incentive for good behavior."

"But this lady told Lisa that she'd used the secret seat for years!" Tim protested.

"The theory of evolution has also been around for years," Larry pointed out, "but that doesn't mean that it's a reasonable theory. Stupid ideas sometimes take a long while to die out."

Tim was silent, feeling a bit deflated at Larry's response to what he saw as a good idea.

"Do you know what usually happens in classes where they use the 'secret seat' idea?"

Tim sighed. "What?"

"The teacher usually ends up giving the prize to the kid in the 'secret seat,' whether or not he's been good! It's pretty hard to tell a kid, 'I'm sorry, but you've been too bad to get the prize.' So the teacher gives the prize even though the kid doesn't deserve it! It becomes a matter of luck rather than a matter of good behavior."

"That makes sense," Tim grudgingly admitted.

"Tim, I'm not trying to throw cold water on a good idea," his friend asserted, "but I've tried the 'secret seat' idea for myself, and I quickly saw why it's not effective. You're a lot better off simply to tell the kids you're looking for the best-behaved kids. If they work for the award, they win it whether they're in a lucky seat or not. That's the simplest way, and it's always the most effective."

Tim laughed. "I'll take your word for it, Edwards. So scratch that *new* idea!"

"While we're on the subject of behavior awards," Larry said, "there's one that I probably haven't mentioned. But it can be very effective, won't take any work on your part, and won't cost you a dime."

"Sounds good," Tim replied. "Tell me about it."

"Reward the well-behaved students with special privileges," Larry explained.

"Special privileges? Like what?"

"Ushering for the offering, helping with the visualized songs, stuff like that."

"You're kidding! Kids will work for that?"

"They will if you present it right," Larry answered. "Conclude your behavior announcement by saying, 'In a few minutes I'm going to need four quiet boys to help take up the offering. Mr. Anderson will be watching, and he'll let me know who the four quiet boys are. I'll also need four quiet girls at the end of Children's Church to pass out the Bible-reading slips, and Mrs. Anderson will be choosing those quiet girls.'"

"And the kids will try to be a winner just for something like that?"

"Sure! As long as you present the job as a special privilege, something that you have to earn by being well behaved."

Tim shook his head. "I never would have thought of that!"

Larry laughed. "It works. Try it. You can have kids help with songs and other visuals, take the offering, run a projector or video, pass out materials, take a report to the church office, and honk the horn for the Bible game. The kids love it; it gets them involved in your teaching ministry; and it becomes an excellent behavior incentive."

"And it doesn't cost a dime."

Larry laughed again. "Right! Hey, Brother, see you tomorrow at work."

So, to be effective, you must...

Prepare.

Use visuals.

Reward good behavior.

Perry Pedagogue

Since we've started using behavior awards in Children's Church...

classroom behavior has improved so dramatically...

that Pastor has decided to use behavior awards in the adult classes!

LET'S CHUCK THE "SECRET SEAT" IDEA!

Miss Ima Spinster stood before her class of Primaries and announced, "Boys and girls, hands in your laps, feet on the floor, sit up straight, look straight ahead, and no talking! Today we're going to have a secret seat winner!

"Before class started, I chose a special seat as our secret seat. At the end of class today, I will tell you which seat is the secret seat. If the boy or girl sitting in that seat has been quiet, I will reward him or her with a special prize! Everyone, sit very quietly, because we just don't know who's sitting in the secret seat. It might be you, and you could win the special prize!"

At the close of the Sunday school hour, Miss Spinster reluctantly presented the prize to the girl sitting in the secret seat, even though the child had been rather disruptive. *I don't want to hurt her feelings*, she told herself. Then she wondered why the secret seat award never seemed to make much difference in the behavior of her class.

THE SECRET SEAT idea has never been effective as a incentive to good behavior in class. Rather than selecting a lucky seat in advance, simply inform your class that you are watching for the quietest student in class and that student will win the behavior award. Good behavior will result!

EVALUATING OUR BEHAVIOR AWARDS

YES   NO

___   ___   1. Do we make the awards on an individual basis?

___   ___   2. Do we base them solely on behavior in class?

___   ___   3. Do we keep the rules to a minimum?

___   ___   4. Do we base the number of winners on the size of the class?

___   ___   5. Are we completely impartial in selecting the winners?

___   ___   6. Do we include both the "church kids" and the "bus kids"?

___   ___   7. Do we use behavior-award games, rather than simply handing out prizes?

___   ___   8. Do we use variety in our behavior-award games?

___   ___   9. Do we keep a written record of the games we have used?

___   ___   10. Do we also reward good behavior by allowing quiet kids to serve as volunteers?

Swapper Shopper   Balloon Bust   FABULOUS FISHING

Beanbag Toss   Let's Make a Deal

Crazy Cube   Mystery Toss   THE MAD DASH

Ask Andy!

Dear Andy,

We would like to use behavior-award games and prizes in our Children's Church program, but the Sunday school superintendent says that there's no money in the budget for that type of thing. (Our church finances are always tight.)

How can we talk him into allocating the funds we need for this?

Robin Banks

Dear Robin,

If church finances are tight, why not consider buying the behavior prizes yourself? (Don't use your tithe money.) The church doesn't have to buy everything; you are allowed to spend your own money.

If you have a faithful crew of Children's Church workers, talk with them about chipping in together to purchase the prizes; or get permission from your pastor to use your Children's Church offerings for this project, then have an offering contest to generate excitement among the students.

Your friend,

Andy

Dear Andy,

We have a boy in Children's Church, Ben Goode, who is a regular terror. He disrupts the program every week, and he drives our workers crazy.

*Anyway, last week we were playing **The Mad Dash**, and I could tell that Ben wanted desperately to win. The improvement in his behavior was incredible! He did fidget just a bit from time to time, but he was trying his best. For Ben it was a major improvement.*

Toward the end of the service, I pointed him out to one of the workers who was serving as a secret agent. She just shrugged and replied that another boy had done even better. She chose one of the church kids, a boy who wins about every third week!

Ben was so disappointed. After church he asked me, "How come I didn't win, Mr. Newtix? I've been good!"

My question is this: Shouldn't we have taken into account the fact that Ben was really trying? He wasn't perfect, of course, but his behavior that day was a huge improvement over the norm!

Herman Newtix

Dear Herman,

I agree. When a normally disruptive child is making an all-out effort to improve, he or she needs to be noticed and commended. Sometimes we need to take the background of the student into consideration as we select our behavior winners. When a child gives the very best of which he is capable, yet still does not win, he can very easily become discouraged and figure there's no use in trying. His behavior may deteriorate drastically at that point.

This is not something I recommend on a regular basis, but you might want to consider giving Ben a small gift before Children's Church next week and telling him that you appreciated his desire to improve. Just the fact that you noticed will do wonders.

Andy

Dear Andy,

The song leader in our Children's Church uses the overhead projector to project the words to the songs (I guess you call them the lyrics) on the screen. But he always insists on turning off the lights each time so that the kids can see the screen better.

Is this really necessary? It creates a distraction each time he asks somebody to get the lights, and the dark room makes it harder for our workers to see the kids. What do you think?

Charlotte Swebb

Dear Charlotte,

Overhead projectors were designed for use with the room lights on. Your song leader really shouldn't have to turn the lights off every time he uses the projector. I can just imagine the distractions this would cause.

If your projector seems especially dim, carefully clean the lenses, mirrors, and fresnel lens to make sure that you are getting the maximum output from your machine. You might even consider purchasing a newer, brighter projector. (Check the specs on the machine to find out how many lumens it produces before you purchase it.)

Another possibility: If there is a light fixture directly over the screen, replace the bulbs with a lower wattage. If you use the overhead extensively in your services, consider temporarily disabling the fixture before class by loosening one of the bulbs.

You want the brightest image possible on the screen, but switching the lights on and off throughout the service could be a major distraction.

Andy

4.

CLUTTERED CLASSROOMS CAUSE CONFUSION AND CHAOS

Tim and Larry stepped back and admired the finished *Balloon Bust Board*. "Looks pretty good, if I do say so myself," Larry announced. "Your kids will like it."

"Debbie did a good job on the border," Tim replied. "Be sure to thank her for us. And thank you for your help. Lisa and I both appreciate the interest you've taken in our Children's Church ministry. We'd be lost without your help."

"Glad to do it," Larry responded. "Children's ministries are so important, and we'll do anything we can to help you do your very best."

Gripping the four-by-six board with both hands, Tim lifted it and started for his car, then set it down again. "Wait a second! This won't fit in the Lexus! How will I get it down to church?"

"Let's throw it in the back of my van, and I'll take it down for you. Will there be anyone at the church to let us in?"

After a quick phone call to locate a church key, Tim and Larry drove to the church. The assistant pastor unlocked the door for them, then disappeared into his office.

"Well, this is it," Tim said, flipping on the light switch as he and Larry carried the board into the room. The two men leaned the balloon board against a wall. Larry turned and silently surveyed the room.

Large flakes of ugly gray paint were peeling from the dirty, dismal walls. Brown stains on the ceiling tiles overhead gave evidence of many years of leaking roofs, and two of the six light bulbs in the room were burned out. A cluster of broken chairs huddled forlornly in one corner beside a broken air-conditioning unit and boxes of ancient Sunday school material. Attendance charts from bygone years competed for space on the walls with yellowing revival announcements, Vacation Bible School posters, and even a yard sale advertisement. One of the two windows at the front of the room sported yellowing, stained curtains, while the other was quite bare.

Larry shook his head. "So this is where you teach, huh? This room needs help!"

Tim was surprised. "What's wrong with it?"

His friend pointed to one of the VBS posters. "It's from 1992! Tim, your classroom should help your teaching, not hinder it. This room is like a dungeon! It's dark, cluttered, and desperately needs a coat of paint and some new curtains. Right now this place has a depressing atmosphere and sends out an unmistakable message that nobody cares."

Tim raised his eyebrows. "That bad, huh?"

"I wouldn't want to have to teach in here. A classroom in this condition is actually working against you every time you occupy it. Spruce up the place a bit, and your teaching situation will automatically improve."

"You're kidding!"

"Not really. Tim, the condition of the classroom is of greater importance than most teachers realize. Some of our discipline problems arise as a result of the room situation. Let's see what we can do to brighten up this place a bit."

Larry isn't exaggerating—the condition of your classroom is very important. A dark, dreary or cluttered classroom actually hinders your teaching ministry, while a bright, cheery room that's kept neat and tidy helps create a positive teaching situation. Your classroom is more important than you might think.

Check out your own classroom. Consider the lighting, the cleanliness of the room and fixtures, the placement of the doors and windows, the arrangement of the rows of chairs. Do improvements need to be made?

Perhaps some changes would improve the efficiency of your teaching and therefore improve classroom discipline. Many times teachers fail to realize just how much influence the classroom setting can have on the students' attention and behavior. Make your classroom work for you *instead* of against you.

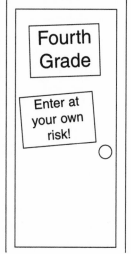

"So what needs to be changed?" Tim asked. "I know the room is a bit dark and dreary, but I'm not even sure where to start."

"I'll make a list," Larry replied, sitting down and scribbling some notes on the back of a handout he picked up from the floor. Minutes later, he handed the following list to Tim:

Improvements needed:

1. Paint walls
2. New curtains
3. Replace ceiling tiles
4. Remove broken chairs, a/c unit, S.S. materials
5. Replace 50-watt bulbs with 100-watt
6. Turn chairs to face long wall
7. New posters and room decorations

A look of surprise crossed Tim's face as he scanned through the list. "This is gonna be a lot of work!"

"Not that much," Larry responded. "And it will change the entire appearance of this room."

"But is it really that important?" Tim queried.

Larry nodded. "It will tell your kids that you really care; it will tell the parents and other church members that this is an important ministry; and, of course, you'll be doing it for your Lord, who deserves your best."

He looked at his watch. "Tell you what, Tim. This project is important enough that I'll volunteer to help you with it tomorrow. You buy the paint and the ceiling tiles, and I'll help you until four o'clock when I have to do some final polishing on my lesson. I think I can speak for Debbie and promise that she'll make curtains."

"But what if the church doesn't want to pay for the paint and stuff?"

"You buy it," Larry told him. "Save the receipt and give it to your pastor if you wish, but if the church doesn't want to reimburse you, you've made a small investment in an important ministry."

Tim shrugged. "Okay. Nine o'clock tomorrow?"

Larry nodded.

Tim glanced at the list again. "Bigger light bulbs?"

"You have fifty-watters in now," Larry answered, "but these fixtures will safely take hundred-watters. You only have four good bulbs, which gives you a total of two hundred watts. If we replace all six, that'll jump you to six hundred watts! It's better to teach in a bright classroom."

Tim pointed at the sixth item on the list. "Turn chairs to face long wall? Why?"

"Right now your students are facing those two windows," Larry replied, "which happen to be on the east wall. The glare from the morning sun must make it hard for your kids to see your visuals. If we turn the class to face the side wall, the windows will be to one side, which is far better.

"That will also place the classroom doors behind your class, instead of at the side. Late-comers and kids going to the bathroom will be less of a distraction.

"But best of all, you're going from six rows of chairs to four, which brings the kids that much closer to you and your visual aids. I've found that the closer the kids are, the more involved they get. It's a psychological thing."

Tim shook his head. "You think of everything."

Larry shrugged. "Your room is important, Tim. I'm just trying to show you how to make it work for you instead of against you."

"I'll call Pastor tonight," Tim said, "and make sure we have permission to paint and make the changes you suggest."

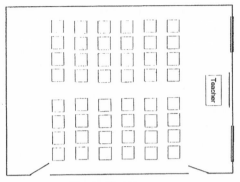

Tim's Classroom

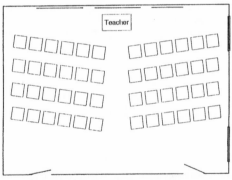

Larry's Suggested Arrangement

Larry nodded as the two men headed for the door. "Good idea. And one more thing. We'll need to move the chalkboard before we paint. Why don't we just replace it with a dry erase board? They're a lot nicer."

Is your classroom working for you or against you? Some classrooms actually create discipline problems for the teacher, but simple changes can eliminate many of the problems. Here are some things to check for:

1. **Placement of doors and windows.** Do your students face the

classroom door, which creates a major distraction every time it opens? Why not turn the chairs so that the door is behind your students, or at least on the side?

It's best not to have your class facing windows with the glare and the distraction of people walking by. If it's not possible to rearrange the chairs, placing the windows to the side, then invest in some blinds or solar film.

2. **Lighting**. Your classroom needs to be bright and cheery. Be diligent to replace any blown bulbs and have any non-working fixtures repaired. Step up to higher wattage bulbs, if necessary. If your room has dark, depressing walls, get permission to paint them a lighter color.

If your room has any fluorescent fixtures that flicker or buzz, be sure to replace them immediately! These can be major distractions.

I like a happy classroom!

Lighting is so important. I've noticed in my public school assemblies that if the auditorium, cafeteria or gymnasium in which I am conducting the program is bright and cheery, the students respond easily to my presentation, and discipline is good. But if the area is dark and dreary, with a gloomy atmosphere, it's harder to hold the attention of the students, and discipline problems can result.

3. **Placement of chairs**. As Larry told Tim, it's best to have fewer

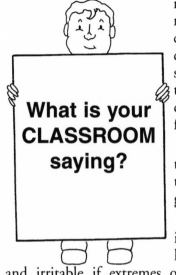

What is your CLASSROOM saying?

rows, with more chairs in each row. If your room is a rectangle rather than a square, consider placing the chairs so that your students face the long wall rather than the shorter one. Keep in mind that you want the doors to the rear, if possible, with windows to the rear or sides, or covered with film and blinds if they must be in front.

If you can arrange your room so that the students face the longest wall, doors are to the rear, and windows to the sides, you've got it made!

4. **Room temperatures**. How often this important detail is overlooked! Children get restless and irritable if extremes of temperature make them uncomfortable.

Last month I spoke in a church near Washington, D.C. We had about seventy kids in a large room that was stifling hot. I discovered after the service that there was only one air-conditioning vent in the entire room. It was a two-by-ten-inch ceiling vent at the far end of the room!

When I mentioned the heat to the Children's Church leader, he responded, "Yes, it's always hot in here."

When the classroom is too warm, it's harder for your students to pay attention. They get restless. Discipline problems are sure to follow.

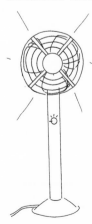

Keep a close eye on the thermostat. Try to be sure that your room is cooled down ahead of time in the warm months. But if you don't have adequate cooling, at least invest in some quiet, oscillating fans. Even in a room that's a bit too warm, your students can still be comfortable if you keep the air moving.

In the winter months, check ahead of time to make sure that the heat is on. Bring a couple of space heaters to class if you have a classroom that is always chilly. In the event that the building custodian insists on keeping the heat too high, you may want to get out the fans again!

A classroom that is too hot or too cold makes the students uncomfortable, and that leads to inattention and discipline problems.

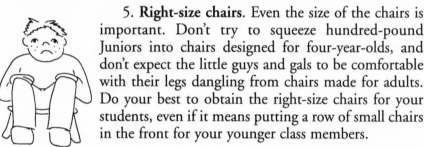

5. **Right-size chairs**. Even the size of the chairs is important. Don't try to squeeze hundred-pound Juniors into chairs designed for four-year-olds, and don't expect the little guys and gals to be comfortable with their legs dangling from chairs made for adults. Do your best to obtain the right-size chairs for your students, even if it means putting a row of small chairs in the front for your younger class members.

6. **Get rid of clutter!** Your classroom should not resemble the tail end of a yard sale, nor should the walls be the community bulletin board. Remove any broken chairs (or other furniture), and get permission to move that ancient copier to a storage area. If there is a furnace or other eyesore that for some reason cannot be evicted from

your classroom, consider hiding it behind a portable screen. Be sure to clear the walls of clutter, replacing those posters left ten years ago by the senior adult class with some bright Scripture posters designed for kids.

Your classroom is important!

"The place looks totally different!" Tim exclaimed as he finished straightening the last of the chairs. "New coat of paint, new ceiling tiles, and brighter light bulbs. Looks good, doesn't it?"

Larry smiled as he consulted his watch. "It looks really good, Tim. And we finished with a half hour to spare."

"Lisa's gonna shop for some bright posters and wall decorations to make the place even cheerier," Tim announced. "And once we have Debbie's curtains up, the kids won't even recognize the place! Hey, thanks again for your help."

Larry studied the rows of chairs. "How many kids did you have last Sunday?"

"Thirty-one," Tim replied. "They now have the fours and fives in another class."

Larry nodded. "Good. Hey, how about if we remove the last row of chairs?"

Tim frowned. "What for?"

"Three rows give you thirty-six seats. If we eliminate the last row, you'll have all the kids closer to you. You can add the extra row again as your Children's Church grows and you need the seats."

Tim nodded thoughtfully, then began folding chairs. "I can't wait until the kids see this room tomorrow," he said with a grin. "That dismal dungeon we had for a classroom is gone forever!"

So, to be effective, you must...

Prepare.

Use visuals.

Reward good behavior.

Spruce up your classroom.

Perry Pedagogue

I've gotta do something about this classroom! We put up with leaky pipes...

And spiders, and roaches, and bugs. Fortunately, we no longer have rats –

They were eaten by the snake under the stairs!

Evaluating My Classroom Setting

YES NO

___ ___ 1. Are the seats positioned so that the class-room doors are to the rear?

___ ___ 2. Are the windows to the side and/or rear?

___ ___ 3. If the windows are in front, have we elimi-nated the glare with blinds and/or solar film?

___ ___ 4. Is the room properly lit?

___ ___ 5. Is it bright and cheery?

___ ___ 6. Do we promptly replace any buzzing or flickering lights?

___ ___ 7. Do I have as few rows of chairs as possible, so that the children are as close as possible?

___ ___ 8. Are the chairs the right size for my pupils?

___ ___ 9. Do I keep the room at a comfortable tem-perature?

___ ___ 10. Is the room clean and neat?

___ ___ 11. Are the furniture and equipment in good repair?

___ ___ 12. Is the room cheerfully decorated?

Ask Andy!

Dear Andy,

I asked my husband about getting a fan for my Sunday school classroom, so he brought a giant fan from his shop. The thing is over three feet across, and rumbles like a freight train. I have to shout to teach over the noise, and it puts out enough wind to straighten any permanent.

How do I tell him that his fan is not what I had in mind? The U.S. Weather Service would issue storm warnings if they ever walked by my classroom!

Gail Force

Dear Gail,

Don't be too hard on the man—he was trying to help.

Fans can help make a classroom comfortable, but you should never have to compete with them to be heard. Go to your local discount store (i.e., Wal-Mart) and purchase a couple of quiet fans. (Have a clerk plug one in so you can hear it running before you make your purchase.) And of course, the best time of year to buy fans is at the end of the summer season when the stores put them on sale.

When you put the fans in your classroom, try to position them so that they are not blowing directly on a student.

By the way, would you like an application for membership in my FAN CLUB?

Best wishes,

Andy

Dear Andy,

I have a kid in my AWANA Club who sits by the window and plays with the blinds all through Council Time. I've told him and told him to leave them alone, but he just doesn't listen. What should I do?

Alan Rench

Dear Alan,

Move the kid! Seat him on the center aisle or next to a worker, but keep him away from the window. You're in charge!

Andy

Dear Andy,

When we are counseling children at the invitation, our Children's Church director tells us to leave the door to the counseling room open just a few inches, rather than closing it to shut out noise and distractions. He insists that we do this to protect ourselves and our ministry against accusations of misconduct with the children.

Is it really necessary to be this cautious?

Lena Ginster

Dear Lena,

Your Children's Church director is right—we have to be extremely cautious when dealing with children. In today's society, anyone accused of an impropriety with a child is guilty until proven innocent, especially if the accused is a church-goer!

The ideal situation when counseling children is to have at least two adults in the room at all times. When two or more groups of children are being counseled in the same classroom, have each group turn their chairs to face a corner of the room, thus placing the counselees' backs to any other activity or distraction in the room.

If you must counsel a child alone, by all means, leave the door open to protect yourself and your ministry! This applies especially when you are dealing with discipline problems.

I'm aware of a situation in which a bus parent accused Beginner Church teachers of molesting her children. The detective assigned to the case was able to get the charges dropped after he became convinced that the ladies involved were innocent and that the church had done everything possible to be certain that such an incident could not take place. He advised the church to drop that family's apartment building from their bus route. (As it turned out, the accusations were a smoke screen—the mother was the one molesting the children!)

Take every precaution possible to protect yourself and your church.

Andy

Dear Andy,

Recently I was told that churches need to have signed permission slips to baptize children! This seems incredible, but is it true?

Aaron C. Rescue

Dear Aaron,

Your underage daughter can get an abortion without your permission, but the church had better not baptize her without your permission! Incredible as it seems, it's true: to protect our ministries, we do need signed permission slips to baptize children. Churches in at least two states have faced multimillion-dollar lawsuits because they baptized bus kids without the parent's signature on the dotted line. In fact, the Christian Law Association recommends getting signed permission slips to baptize members' children!

The sample permission form on page 94 was provided courtesy of CLA. If you have further questions, contact them at the following address:

Christian Law Association
P. O. Box 4010
Seminole, FL 33775–4010

Don't forget to pray for the folks at CLA, and your church may want to consider supporting them financially. They are providing a valuable service to churches, ministries and families across this nation.

For the children,

Andy

Christian Law Association *Liability Release Forms*

SAMPLE FORM C

Bus Rider Attendance and Baptism Permission Form

I. We are a Baptist church.

II. We believe the Bible is God's Word.

III. Our purpose: (Matthew 28:19, 20)

    A.   To present the Gospel
1. We are all sinners. (Romans 3:10)
2. The price for sin is to die and spend eternity in hell. (Romans 6:23)
3. Jesus died to pay for our sin. (Romans 5:8).
4. Anyone who will call on Jesus and trust Him to be saved, will be saved. (Romans 10:13).

    B.   Baptize
We give everyone who makes a profession of faith in Christ an opportunity to be baptized as is found in Acts 2:38, 41.

    C.   Teach the Bible
After a person trusts Christ and is baptized, we teach him or her how to have God's blessings on his life by obeying and living by the principles in the Bible.

I understand the purpose and beliefs of the _____ Church. I also understand that unless otherwise noted, the child who is listed below will be given an opportunity to follow the Lord in believer's baptism if and when he trusts Christ as his or her Savior. Understanding this, I give my permission for the child listed below to attend church, to be taught the Bible, and to be baptized if he accepts Christ as Savior.

My child _____ has my permission to ride the bus to attend
_____ Church.

My child also has my permission to be baptized if he accepts Christ as his or her Savior.

I wish to be present at his baptism.   Yes _____ No _____

Special Instructions concerning my child:

_____

_____

_____   _____
Parent's Signature   Date

5.

EVERYONE ENJOYS ENERGETIC, EXCITED ENTHUSIASM!

Tim had just finished putting his lesson visuals in order and was checking on the visualized songs when several classes came flooding in to join the third graders. "Whoa!" exclaimed Justin, a noisy, energetic fourth grader. "What happened to this place?"

"Why are the chairs turned sideways?" asked Mandie, a cute, blond, little seven-year-old.

"This room looks new!" exclaimed one of the third-grade students. "It looks like a happy room now. I like it!"

The posters and room decorations weren't purchased yet, and the naked windows still waited anxiously for their new curtains, but the room did look better—much better! Catching just a bit of her husband's enthusiasm, Lisa Wellington had whipped out some banners on her computer. WELCOME TO CHILDREN'S CHURCH! the one across the front of the room proclaimed in five-inch letters. A smaller font beneath it declared, WE'RE GLAD YOU'RE HERE!

Several one-page signs read, CALVARY BAPTIST CHURCH LOVES KIDS! and a banner across the back of the room announced, JESUS LOVES YOU, AND SO DO WE!

An unusual thrill of excitement swept over Tim as he stepped to the front to open the service. "Good morning!" he called in a cheerful voice that radiated warmth and enthusiasm. "We're glad you're here! Let's all stand and sing 'This Is the Day'! Mr. Anderson will lead us, and then I want to tell you about something really special!"

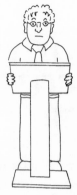

Enthusiasm is contagious. Every time you stand to teach, give it everything you've got. Kids enjoy listening to a teacher who radiates warmth, excitement, energy and enthusiasm. On the other hand, the slow-moving, quiet-mannered teacher who drones on and on in a monotone will lose the attention of any class, no matter how good the material he is presenting.

Teach with enthusiasm! Teach with excitement! Put every ounce of energy you possess into your presentation. Teach with such intensity, such earnestness, such urgency that your students are compelled to listen.

You may be saying, "But that's just not me. I'm kind of quiet and laid back, and I never show excitement about anything. It would be totally out of character for me to act enthused and excited."

Then ask God to give you the enthusiasm you lack! He can do it!

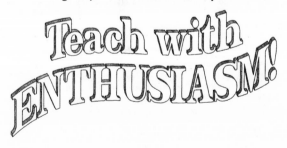

96

By nature, I am a quiet, laid-back sort of person. I'm an introvert. Even today it's hard for me to walk into a room and introduce myself to three strangers. It's just the way I'm wired.

But I've learned the importance of projecting enthusiasm, and I can walk into an auditorium or gymnasium with a thousand kids and capture the attention of the entire crowd in the first ten seconds. I asked God for it, and He taught me how.

So get excited! Teach with enthusiasm and lots of energy! You'll soon learn that you can hold the attention of your students just with the force and intensity of your presentation.

You may be thinking, *But this is just the energy of the flesh, and it's artificial. We're supposed to operate in the power of the Spirit.*

You're missing the point. We, as teachers of God's Word, have got to be praying, totally yielded, dependent upon the power of the Spirit of God. Anything done in the energy of the flesh is useless, and actually distasteful to God, but God can use excited, energetic people! Ask Him to equip you with the enthusiasm you need.

Which would you rather hear?

Put yourself in the student's chair. Would you rather listen to a speaker who drones along in a dull monotone, stands in one place with no change of facial expression or use of gestures, and never makes eye contact with you? Or would you rather listen to a lively, friendly speaker who is so charged with enthusiasm and excitement that his eagerness compels you to listen? Other things being equal, which speaker would be more effective in the presentation of the Gospel and teaching of the Word of God?

Here are several tools that God has given you to use to project enthusiasm and excitement, love and compassion, urgency and concern to your students as you teach them the eternal Word of God:

1. **YOUR EYES**—The eyes of the teacher can be dynamic teaching tools, if he knows how to use them. His eyes can express excitement, enthusiasm and anticipation as he teaches; they can radiate warmth, love and friendliness; they can portray sincerity, eagerness and intense feelings. As he becomes involved with the characters of the Bible story, his eyes can express rage, disappointment, worry, love, hatred, anxiety or compassion.

Learn to look directly into the eyes of the students as you teach. Give each child the impression you are teaching directly to him! Often you can hold the attention of a class simply by practicing good eye contact with each student. What tremendous teaching tools your eyes are! Learn to use them to their full potential.

The eyes of the students are just as important and can provide you with all sorts of information if you are alert enough to pick up the signals. By

Practice good eye contact.

watching your pupils' eyes, you can sense immediately when they are becoming restless and you need a slight change of pace. You can tell when the students are excited, when they are pleased, when they are enjoying class. By observing the questions in a child's eyes, you become aware of the need to rephrase or reword a concept or to explain further.

Use your eyes to communicate your message to the students. Remember: this is a two-way transmission, so be sure to pick up the nonverbal signals they are sending you.

Many times discipline problems can be avoided simply by making eye contact with the student whose attention you have momentarily lost. Are those two little girls on the third row talking again? Simply walk over and stand in front of them as you continue to teach. The moment you make eye contact with one or both of them, shake your head ever so slightly, and they'll get the message. If they don't, quietly correct them.

This is one reason you want the students seated as close to you as possible. Kids don't take up as much space as adults, so place the rows a little closer together. You might be amazed at how much closer the back row suddenly becomes. Your eye contact will improve dramatically as the students are brought closer to you.

2. **YOUR VOICE**—What a powerful, versatile and dynamic teaching tool God gave you when He equipped you with a voice! The human voice has more versatility and possibilities than a grand piano, yet many teachers play it like a child's two-octave keyboard!

That voice box of yours can produce shouts, whispers, grunts, groans, wails, sobs, laughter and shrieks of joy. It can be used to express pain, sorrow, excitement, regret, joy, anger, insecurity, hatred, love, suspicion, enthusiasm, confidence, scorn and admiration. What an instrument! What a tool for capturing and holding attention!

Your voice is a powerful teaching tool!

Ask the Lord to teach you to use your voice to its fullest potential. Never be guilty of teaching in a monotone! Imagine Chopin sitting down to an eleven-foot grand piano with eighty-eight keys, then striking just one key repeatedly in an attempt to play a sonata!

Don't be afraid of allowing your emotions to find their way into your voice as you teach. Your voice should convey a compelling sense of urgency as you present the plan of salvation. Why shouldn't your voice

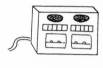 be tinged with anger when you warn your students of modern-day evils? As you teach the blessed story of Calvary, your voice should flag with pain and sorrow, but oh, what joy and excitement as you tell of the resurrection!

Here is a helpful exercise in learning to use your voice to its full capacity: Take a tape recorder to class and record your lesson. Evaluate the effectiveness of your use of your voice as you listen to the tape in the privacy of your home. Do this for several weeks, and you're certain to see marked improvement!

The greatest potential for the effective use of your voice is found in your telling of the Bible story. Even if you don't attempt various voices for the dialogue portions, your voice can express terrifying rage if the speaker is angry. Use your voice to portray fear and anxiety if the speaker is worried. This versatile instrument called the voice can sound notes of joy, sorrow, excitement, hatred, scorn, etc., to express the emotions of the various characters in your Bible stories. What fun you can have just learning to use your voice to hold a crowd of children spellbound as you share the Word of God!

You can shout to regain the lost attention of your students, but you can also drop your voice to a whisper. You can speak rapidly and forcefully to make a point, but you can also speak slowly and distinctly, ONE-WORD-AT-A-TIME-LIKE-THIS, to get your point across. Your voice has an almost endless combination of tones, inflections, speeds and volumes. Learn to use them effectively.

To get an idea of the power of this dynamic teaching tool, listen to an Ethel Barrett story record. You'll be amazed at what can be done with one human voice!

3. **YOUR GESTURES**—Hands can be so expressive! Learn to use them to enhance your message.

Did you realize that your hands, by themselves, can express helplessness, fear, worry, rage, love and many other human emotions and attitudes? Use your hands as you teach!

A word of warning: don't simply allow your hands to flop about and flail the air as you talk. This can be quite distracting and actually detracts from your lesson instead of enhancing it. Have a friend video tape you as you teach. It can be a bit intimidating to view the results, but it provides an honest evaluation!

As you learn to use hand gestures, make them big. Make them bold. Make them with enthusiasm! If you teach a class of thirty, make your gestures big and energetic enough for a class of five hundred!

4. **YOUR FACIAL EXPRESSIONS**—Deaf evangelist Reggie Rempel cannot speak a word of English and presents his message in sign language. His wife, Kim, interprets the message for him by speaking audibly as he signs. I love to hear him preach. Although I cannot read sign language, I understand a great deal of his message even before his wife interprets.

How? Reggie is a master at using facial expressions. His facial expressions sometimes say as much as his words.

Learn to use your facial expressions to enhance your message and hold the attention of your students. We don't usually think of facial expressions as a teaching method, but they are. Used properly, they can be quite effective.

5. **YOUR SMILE**—A warm, friendly smile can do much to convey the message of the Gospel! Children enjoy listening to an amiable teacher who smiles often, rather than having to endure a "sour puss" who never allows them to catch even a glimpse of her teeth as she teaches.

So learn to smile! Practice if you need to, but smile! Children are drawn to a warm, loving teacher, and then are drawn to that teacher's Saviour.

Perhaps nothing conveys enthusiasm and excitement better than a warm smile.

6. **YOUR BODY LANGUAGE**—If you teach children, don't try to do it standing in one place! Get rid of that pulpit or lectern that you

hide behind, and use some body language!

Move about as you speak. Be animated! Use
your entire body to teach! When describing a sinis-
ter character, lean forward and slowly stalk toward
the students as you speak in a low, menacing tone.
If you're talking about the Devil coming with a
temptation, hold your hands up as if for protection
and back slowly away as if attempting to escape a
life-threatening danger. When portraying a joyful,
happy situation (the resurrection, for example),
leap into the air for joy!

Learn to make your gestures BIG. Even if you are teaching a small
class, make your gestures huge, as if you were addressing a huge crowd
in a gymnasium. Remember that gestures are not limited to the hands
alone; use your entire body!

Enthusiastic teaching demands a lot of energy. You'll sometimes go
home on Sunday afternoon totally drained and exhausted, but thrilled
and exhilarated at the fantastic way in which your students responded
to the lesson. Enthusiastic teaching takes work, but it's worth it!

Teach with enthusiasm!

When you think of "body language,"
you can't help but think of the old-time
evangelist Billy Sunday. Now there was a
man who put everything he had into his
messages! He knew how to teach and
preach with enthusiasm.

Billy Sunday would race about on the
platform as he preached, leap into the air,
whirl about, or drop flat on his face. Critics
denounced his preaching style as "vulgar"
and "flamboyant," but no one could deny
that the evangelist was effective! His unusual,
attention-demanding style of preaching
drew huge crowds, and he was used of God
to win thousands to the Saviour.

When Billy Sunday preached about
sin, he did so with an intensity that left no
doubts that he hated it. When he urged lost

sinners to repent and come to the Saviour, hearts were moved by his earnestness and sincerity. When he spoke of the joys of salvation, his exuberance and joy could actually be felt by his listeners. Billy Sunday was a man who preached with enthusiasm.

Ask God to teach you to do the same. Enthusiastic teachers are effective for the Master. Learn to use your eyes, your voice, your hands, your facial expressions, your smile, your entire body to present the message of Christ in such an enthusiastic, compelling manner that your students will be captivated by your zeal and excitement.

Boredom among the students? Inattention and indifference? Discipline problems? They'll become a thing of the past!

* * *

Tim and Lisa Wellington stood at the door of their classroom, shaking hands and saying good-bye as their kids filed out. The eight-year-old Bradford twins came rushing up and, to Tim's surprise and delight, threw their arms around him. "You're a great teacher, Mr. Wellington!" David declared. "I liked your Bible story!"

His sister, Dana, nodded in agreement. "I liked it too!" she announced. David grabbed her sleeve and hurried her toward the bus.

Tim looked at Lisa in surprise. "Two weeks ago," he said softly, "they were our worst kids! I wonder what's come over them."

Lisa smiled. "Maybe they're not the only ones who are changing," she answered mysteriously. "You were really enthusiastic today, and I noticed that the kids really listened. You're enjoying this Children's Church, aren't you?"

Tim grinned. "I'm starting to!"

Teach with enthusiasm! Express it through your...

So, to be effective, you must...

Prepare.

Use visuals.

Reward good behavior.

Spruce up your classroom.

Teach with enthusiasm and excitement.

Perry Pedagogue

I think some teachers get a little too excited. They get too emotional!

As adults, we should have better control!

Go, Stealers! No! NO! Not that way, you idiot!

Am I Excited and Enthusiastic?

YES NO

___ ___ 1. Am I excited about teaching the Word of God and seeing lives changed?

___ ___ 2. Do I enjoy being with my students? Does it show?

___ ___ 3. Do I really give my very best each time I teach?

___ ___ 4. As I teach, do my eyes radiate enthusiasm, sincerity and love for my students?

___ ___ 5. Do I practice good eye contact by looking directly into the eyes of each student?

___ ___ 6. Do I watch the eyes of my students so that I know whether I have their full attention and whether they are understanding the lesson?

___ ___ 7. Do I really understand just how versatile and powerful my voice is as a teaching tool?

___ ___ 8. Do I avoid teaching in a monotone?

___ ___ 9. Do I use my voice to express a variety of emotions?

___ ___ 10. If I am losing the attention of my pupils, do I know at least three ways to use my voice alone (other than raising it) to regain attention?

___ ___ 11. Do I make maximum use of gestures to convey enthusiasm?

___ ___ 12. Do I make maximum use of facial expressions?

___ ___ 13. Do I smile as I teach, conveying the love of the Saviour to each of my students?

___ ___ 14. Do I move about as I teach, rather than standing stiffly in one place?

___ ___ 15. Do I use "body language" to help convey my message?

Ask Andy!

Dear Andy,

By nature, I am an excited, energetic person, and I have no trouble at all projecting enthusiasm in class. But I find that I tend to get the kids too wound up, and then I can't settle them down to listen to the lesson. What would you suggest?

Minnie Vann

Dear Minnie,

Without meeting you I would venture to guess that there are few dull moments in your class. Enthusiastic teachers like you are fun to be around.

But some teachers get their students so "wound up" that they become rowdy: screaming and yelling, etc. Instead, it's best to channel that energy toward class activities that have a purpose: spirited singing, lively memory drills, etc.

And when you're trying to create a slower, quieter atmosphere in preparation for the lesson, try using music. Quiet, slower-paced songs, such as "God Is So Good," "Whisper a Prayer," or "Seek Ye First," can be very effective in settling the students and preparing them to listen quietly. Sing a verse or two, watching the kids closely to determine the effect the song is having; continue singing another verse or two if necessary.

When the class is settled, quietly remind them of your behavior rules, lead them in prayer (in a soft, quiet voice), then jump into your lesson. Open the lesson with a captivating illustration; keep the lesson moving;

and give your presentation every ounce of energy you've got! Your students will listen eagerly.

Andy

Dear Andy,

   I'm just not an enthusiastic-type person. I'm quiet, slow-moving, and really never get excited about anything. In fact, some of the other teachers call me "the robot."

   But I'd like to learn to be energetic and enthusiastic. Is that possible?

Ann Droid

Dear Ann,

Yes, it is possible to learn to project enthusiasm. The very fact that you want to is an excellent indication that you will succeed.

Watch other teachers who are known for their enthusiasm. Listen to tapes of motivational speakers and watch videos of speakers who are effective in holding the attention of a crowd. Then analyze their presentation to determine what makes them effective, and mimic what you see them do. At first it will seem artificial, but after a time, enthusiasm will come naturally. You learned to walk and talk and tie your shoes by watching others; why not learn enthusiasm the same way?

By nature, I am a quiet, laid-back sort of person; but for several years I served under a bus director whose middle name must have been "Enthusiasm." I learned to get excited by watching him.

Andy

Dear Andy,

   What kind of songs do you recommend for children's classes

and worship services? Our song leader in Children's Church uses a lot of chant-type songs. He belts out a line, then the kids repeat it back to him. There's no real melody. By the end of the "song," the kids are not really singing: they're shouting. It just doesn't seem appropriate.

Phil Harmonic

Dear Phil,

I'm afraid there's a lot of inappropriate "music" being used in kids' ministries today, even in fundamental Baptist churches. It should go without saying that rock, rap and contemporary music have no place in the church!

I'm familiar with the "chant" type of song that you refer to, and I agree that it is not conducive to a worshipful service. It seems that more and more ministries are using this type of "music," but it's counter-productive. I've noticed that the teachers who use this type of song usually have problems with discipline in class.

Use songs that emphasize the melody. This type music speaks to the heart and actually prepares the student to listen to God's Word!

While we're on the subject of music, make certain that the songs you use have a clear message. I recently heard a "song" that said: "No, you can't get to Heaven on roller skates; you'll roll right past those pearly gates." What kind of a message is that?

Child Evangelism Fellowship produces some excellent visualized songs that are colorful, melodic and meaningful. You might get your song leader to replace the "chants" with some of these. Music is so important!

Your friend,

Andy

Dear Andy,

So what's wrong with using contemporary music with young

people? In today's world, you have to. Kids and teens won't
come unless you have upbeat music in your program.

Tom Foolery

Dear Tom,

I asked Andy if I could respond to your letter, and he graciously consented. You and I have both been told that we have to use "upbeat" (worldly) music if we want to reach today's young person. But—is that really true?

A number of years ago I served on the staff of a large, independent Baptist church in a western state. We averaged 1,050 to 1,100 in Sunday school. When our pastor died in an accident, we called a man with a lot of personality and charisma.

The new pastor insisted that we needed to lower our standards in order to reach the younger generation. He brought a lot of worldly music in for the teens and college and career classes. He stayed just eighteen short months, took the church to an average attendance of 500, then left. The last time I visited that church they were running around 120 and held their Sunday evening service in a classroom!

On the other hand, my younger brother recently took a pastorate after serving as a youth director in an independent Baptist church for twelve years. God used him to build a very successful youth group. He not only built a large youth group in his church but was also able to hold Bible clubs in two local public high schools! Five of the teens who were saved through one Bible club later graduated from Bible college and went into full-time ministry!

Here's the bottom line: he never succumbed to the pressure to use worldly music. Incidentally, his teen ministry was in southern California!

Kids won't come unless we use junky music? Don't believe that line for a minute! Let's do what's right, and leave the results with God!

For the children,

Ed Dunlop

6.
STORYTELLING SETS THE STAGE FOR SWEET SUCCESS

The greatest Teacher of all time seemed to have had a favorite method of teaching, one which He employed nearly every time He spoke. Whenever a crowd would gather to hear Him—be they laborers, fishermen and housewives, or the more elite groups of scribes, lawyers and the ever-present Pharisees—they were sure to hear Him employ this powerful, life-changing method of teaching.

Storytelling touches hearts and changes lives.

What was the favorite teaching method of Jesus, the Son of God? *Storytelling,* of course.

Storytelling is perhaps the most effective of all the methods of teaching. It's powerful. No other method grabs the attention of the student as quickly or as completely as storytelling. If for some reason my teaching ministry were to be restricted to just one method, without hesitation I would choose storytelling.

This exciting, enjoyable and effective method of teaching touches hearts and changes lives in three basic ways. Storytelling completely captures the **attention** of the student, helps him to **understand** the lesson, and causes him to **remember** what he has heard.

Come to think of it, those are the three basic reasons why every teacher should use visual aids!

There's a fourth powerful benefit of storytelling: The stories help the student **apply** the biblical truth to his own life. The listener relates to the character in the story; and when he sees how the Bible principle affected that character, he easily relates that truth to his own lifestyle.

The Power of a Story

A well-told story...
1. Captures the **attention** of the student.
2. Helps him to **understand** the lesson.
3. Causes him to **remember** it.
4. Leads him to **apply** it to his own life.

"The prophet whipped his donkey to make him go faster," Tim said, his voice edged with excitement, "but it was no use! The poor donkey was terrified, and he was already running for his life!"

Tim leaned forward, and without realizing it, his listeners did the same. "The prophet saw movement in the bushes at the edge of the road, and his heart nearly stopped! And then..." Tim paused for effect, and in that moment he suddenly realized that many of his students were actually holding their breath. "A branch broke with a loud snap that made the prophet jump with fright." Tim dropped his voice to a whisper, and the kids leaned even closer. "He turned and stared hard at the dense undergrowth, wishing with all his heart that he had not disobeyed God."

Tim suddenly raised his voice. "With a loud, terrifying roar, a lion sprang from the bushes!" Several kids jumped at the words, and Tim almost laughed at their reaction.

Every kid is listening, he thought gratefully. *They're really getting into this story!*

"Did you see the kids today during the Bible lesson?" Tim asked Lisa as they stashed visuals in the trunk of the Lexus. "They didn't move! I've never seen kids so quiet!"

"You're becoming quite a storyteller, Mr. Wellington," Lisa happily replied. "You had the kids on the edge of their seats!"

She laughed. "But the kids weren't the only ones. Mr. Anderson was standing in the back taking a head count while you were telling the story of the disobedient prophet. I looked back and saw him standing there with his mouth open, listening. When you finished the story, he remembered what he was doing, but he had to start all over again!"

Tim laughed. "I never thought I'd see this group so quiet," he remarked. "I'm gonna use stories with every message."

Storytelling is a powerful, effective method of teaching, suitable for any audience and every age group. (Remember, Jesus used this method with adults.) A well-told story grabs the attention of each student, helps him understand the Bible truth being presented, enables him to apply it to his own life, and causes him to remember it. What a powerful, life-changing method of teaching!

> "I love stories! I always listen when my teacher tells a Bible story!"

With a little work the average teacher can plan to capture and hold the attention of every student in class by using a combination of two teaching tools: visual aids and storytelling. Develop your skills as a storyteller, and your lesson time will be a delight as your students become quieter and more attentive than you ever thought possible!

Of all the stories that Jesus told, which one is your favorite?

Here are some principles to follow to maximize the effectiveness of your stories:

1. Begin your lesson with a brief story that poses a question or introduces the topic under consideration. This might be a brief incident from your own life, a selection from a book of illustrations, or even one of the visualized, true-life stories that have been so popular. Select a story that will grab the attention of your pupils, keep it brief, and make sure that it relates to the topic at hand.

2. **Build the lesson around a Bible story**. Many teachers today are almost afraid of using stories from the Bible, the greatest source of stories ever. "My students have probably heard every story in the Bible," they say, "and they'll lose interest." Not true! Your students have not heard every story in the Bible, and they haven't heard them told in the way that you will tell them.

Bible stories are superior to any other type of story for several reasons. If it's a Bible story, you know it's a true story, and the details are accurate. Bible stories hold a special appeal for your students; they're different from every other type of story. We want our students to be familiar with the Word of God because God has promised to bless His Word.

3. **Begin any familiar Bible story with a unique opening**. Find a way to tell the story in such an unusual way that your students will not even recognize the story until it is well underway.

> Early one morning, an old, old man climbed up a steep mountain slope. Over his shoulder he carried a sharp ax. He glanced behind him to see three other men following him up the mountainside with axes on their shoulders.

> The old man entered the forest, walked among the trees for a moment, then chose a giant of a tree. "Let's do this one, boys!" he called. The other men hurried over.
>
> Moments later the forest echoed with the ringing sound of axes biting into wood. "Timber!" shouted the old man, and the others leaped clear.
>
> With a crackling, snapping sound, the tall, tall tree slowly began to fall toward the earth. Snapping branches as it fell, the giant tree slammed to the ground with a crash that silenced the birds. The impact shook the ground.
>
> Three of the men clambered atop the fallen giant, then began to lop off its branches with their saws and axes. The other man hurried to the valley below, then quickly returned with two teams of oxen.

Hitching the oxen to the huge log, he carefully dragged it down to the valley.

The old man watched closely as the log began to move. Then, with a satisfied nod, he turned to select another tree.

The old man, of course, is Noah, and the three assistants are Ham, Shem and Japheth. But your students haven't realized that yet, and they're listening in fascination as you share a very familiar Bible story. Without naming the old man or displaying any visuals that would identify the story, you continue your narrative.

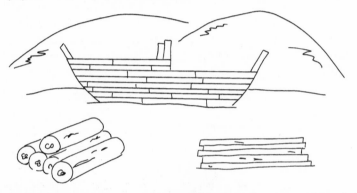

You have the four men cut wood day after day, always stacking it in the valley below. The neighbors are in suspense, wondering what the old man is intending to do with all the wood. Finally, one of them gets up the courage to ask the old man, and learns of his plans to build the ark.

At that point, of course, your students realize that they've been listening to the story of Noah and the ark. But it's too late! They're hooked! You've already gotten them so engrossed in the story that they have to hear you out. Even though they know the ending, they've never heard it like you're going to tell it. And they'll stay with you.

Once the students have identified the story, you begin to use your visuals as you continue.

4. **Prepare your story well.** Study the story in the biblical context, being certain to read any parallel accounts to glean all the details. Outline the story on paper without looking at the text to ascertain that you have the correct sequence of events. Use your imagination to envision the story as it happened, then prepare the story as you saw it. Give personalities to

the characters in the story, and bring them to life for your listeners.

Remember that many of the biblical accounts give just the bare facts of the incident, and you must carefully supply the details. Again, use your imagination. Genesis 6 doesn't even mention Noah's cutting the trees, but we know he must have, so why not include it in the story? We're not told that Japheth hit his thumb with his hammer, but in all those years of building, he must have! Why not add interest to the account by referring to it? (You might even have him drop his hammer in pain, nearly hitting Shem down below, much to the amusement of the scornful neighbors who were watching.)

Study that story until it becomes a part of you and you can tell it flawlessly. Meditate on the account until the characters are as real to you as your next-door neighbors. It takes work, but a good story is worth the effort!

"Then King Solomon said..."

Practice makes perfect!

5. **Practice the story.** Once you have the story constructed in your own mind, practice telling it—aloud—with gestures, voice techniques, facial expressions and body language. Put your all into it, and tell it from beginning to end as if you were in front of five hundred children.

If you're a bit self-conscious about others' overhearing you (I always am), then go off into the woods or some other place where you can be alone, and then give it all you have! (That twenty-five-minute morning commute might be an excellent time to practice your story, but be careful with the gestures and body language. Don't get so involved in the story that you forget that you're the one in control of the car!)

Practice the entire lesson, from the opening illustrations, through the Bible story, to the application and conclusion. Late Saturday afternoon, run through the entire process one more time. If it goes well, you'll have a hard time waiting for Sunday to come!

6. **Use visual aids to enhance your story.** When you combine the power of visuals with an effective, well-told story, you have a winning

combination! Stories grab and hold attention. Good visual aids do the same. So when you put the two together, you can expect an effective presentation!

Use VARIETY in your visuals!

Remember that visuals do not have to be elaborate. The simplest of visual aids can add to the impact of your story. Objects are very practical here, and remember, of course, that visuals are most effective when there is variety.

7. **Be sure to apply the story.** Don't simply tell the story and then leave it hanging. Make application to the lives of your students. Help them to see clearly how the truth of God's Word applies to their own lives. And, of course, be sure to visualize the application as well as the Bible story.

If you've presented a salvation story, why not make application by presenting the plan of salvation step by step from the book of Romans? If you're teaching on the importance of reading God's Word, why not "assign" a passage for each day of the coming week? If the lesson is on witnessing, drive it home by giving each child two or three gospel tracts along with the encouragement to give them to friends or relatives that very week.

8. **Don't try to "force" an application**. Did you ever hear a teacher teach the story of David and Goliath, then try to make a salvation application? The story teaches a number of truths and can be applied many different ways, but the plan of salvation is not one of them.

It could be used to emphasize God's power, trust in God, the fact that God uses young people, our responsibility to stand for right, etc., but to try to make this remarkable story teach salvation by "forcing" the application is a mistake.

Never try to "force" the application.

If you are preaching and teaching on salvation, why not present the story of Adam and Eve, the serpent in the wilderness (concluding with a brief visit to John 3), the Passover, the story of Naaman, Calvary, or even Noah and the ark (emphasizing the folly of waiting)? The Scriptures are filled with stories that clearly teach salvation (or whatever topic you're dealing with). Be sure that the story you select actually teaches what you are intending it to teach!

Would you use the story of the fall of Jericho to teach tithing? Of course not, but it could be done if you're willing to stretch and "force" the application! Before teaching any Bible story, study it carefully to ascertain that it is the appropriate one to present the truth your students need.

If your lesson is on soul winning, honesty, obedience to parents, or some other topic other than salvation, why not present the plan of salvation in a short, separate segment before the Bible lesson? In fact, unless you have a small group and KNOW FOR CERTAIN that every class member has received Christ as Saviour, you would do well to present the plan of salvation in every class session!

How many times I've heard teachers present a lesson that did not even mention the gospel message, then turn around and give a salvation invitation! No wonder children are sometimes confused!

9. **Use storytelling in combination with other teaching methods.** The effectiveness of storytelling is greatly enhanced when it is used with other methods such as lecture, question and answer, role-playing and discussion. This adds variety to your presentation, which helps hold the attention of your students.

Storytelling is undoubtedly the most effective method of teaching available. It has life-changing potential because it captivates **attention**, creates **understanding**, causes students to **remember**, and culminates in **personal application**. Develop your skills as a storyteller so that boredom, indifference and inattention won't stand a chance in your classroom!

Tim sighed and glanced over at Larry as the regional vice president droned on and on with his motivational lecture. *Larry's as bored as I am,* **he thought,** *so it's not just me. This guy is as dry as a dust storm in the Sahara!* **He glanced at his watch, then realized that it displayed exactly the same time as the last time check.**

When the meeting was finally dismissed, both men hurried toward the doors with a sense of relief. "He may be a vice president, but he's no public speaker," Tim remarked as they strode down the hallway. "That was one long half hour!"

"But you have to admit he knew his stuff," Larry replied. "He rattled off facts and figures like he was reciting his address and phone number. And the ideas he presented on cost-cutting measures made sense."

"But he didn't know how to present it," Tim argued. "That was one boring presentation!"

"It was pretty dry," Larry admitted. "He could use a course in public speaking."

"Or two or three of them."

"There's one simple thing he could do to dress up his presentation," Larry said. "He should have shared a few stories! With as many years as he has with the company, he's bound to have had a number of experiences that would make appropriate illustrations. A few relevant stories would have gotten his points across far more effectively."

"I'm learning that in my Children's Church," Tim replied.

"Storytelling is effective," Larry declared. "Well-told stories make the lesson more interesting for your students. They increase your students' comprehension of the material, help them integrate the truth into their lives, and cause them to recall the lesson more readily."

"Storytelling is quickly becoming my favorite method of teaching."

"You're in good company," Larry told him. "It was the favorite method of Jesus too."

So, to be effective, you must...

Prepare.
Use visuals.
Reward good behavior.
Spruce up your classroom.
Teach with enthusiasm and excitement.
Captivate attention by using relevant stories.

Perry Pedagogue

Storytelling

1. **Begin your lesson with a brief story.**

2. **Build the lesson around a Bible story.**

3. **Begin any familiar Bible story with a unique opening.**

4. **Prepare your story well.**

5. **Practice the story.**

6. **Use visual aids.**

7. **Be sure to apply the story.**

8. **Don't try to force an application.**

9. **Use storytelling in combination with other teaching methods.**

Storytelling:

!

It's Powerful!

Which stories teach which truths?

Draw a line from the Bible story on the left to the Bible truth on the right that it can be used to illustrate. (Some stories will have more than one application.)

David & Goliath	Obedience
The fiery furnace	Judgment
Jonah	God uses people
Adam & Eve	Consequences of sin
Feeding the 5,000	Standing for right
Serpent in the wilderness	Trust in God
Jairus' daughter	God's power
Resurrection of Lazarus	Missions
The burning bush	Salvation
Walls of Jericho	Dedication
Naaman the leper	Faithfulness
Peter's jailbreak	Confession of sin
The disobedient prophet	Forgiveness
The prodigal son	God's promises
Calvary	Prayer

Remember: when you select a Bible story, be sure that it illustrates the truth you are teaching! If not, select one that does!

Bible Stories That Teach

Under each Bible topic, list 3 Bible stories that could be used to illustrate it.

SALVATION
1. _____
2. _____
3. _____

GOD'S FAITHFULNESS
1. _____
2. _____
3. _____

CONSEQUENCES OF SIN
1. _____
2. _____
3. _____

NEED FOR PRAYER
1. _____
2. _____
3. _____

WITNESSING
1. _____
2. _____
3. _____

DEDICATION
1. _____
2. _____
3. _____

A good story grabs the child's attention, conveys truth in an enjoyable, interesting way, and makes a lasting impression upon his heart.

EVALUATING MY STORYTELLING TECHNIQUES

YES NO

1. Do I recognize the power of the storytelling method to hold the attention of my students?

2. Do I usually introduce my lesson with a brief illustration or story?

3. Do I usually build the lesson around a Bible story?

4. Do I know how to begin a familiar Bible story with a unique opening to captivate attention?

5. Do I prepare my story well, practicing it until it becomes a part of me?

6. Do I know how to bring the characters to life?

7. Do I use visual aids in the telling of the story?

8. Do I use my voice to its fullest potential in the telling of the story?

9. Do I use facial expressions, gestures, and "body language"?

10. Do I apply the story to the lives of my students?

11. Do I know how to use storytelling in combination with other methods for maximum impact and effectiveness?

12. Do I enjoy storytelling?

13. Can I captivate the attention of my class by telling a story?

Storytelling It's Powerful

Ask Andy!

Dear Andy,

I've been told that it's not appropriate to use incidents from one's own life as illustrations in a lesson or message. Is this true?

Al Pine

Dear Al,

I strongly disagree. Personal illustrations are often the most effective, provided, of course, that they are relevant to the theme of the lesson.

Andy

Dear Andy,

I personally feel that storytelling is a frivolous method of teaching. I see it basically as a waste of time used by teachers who have to fill an allotted period of time in class but are too lazy to prepare an effective lesson. The way I see it, I'm in class to teach, not to entertain.

M. T. Head

Dear M. T.,

I trust that you have an open mind and will take a second look at the storytelling method. The Master Teacher, the Lord Jesus Himself, did not see storytelling as a frivolous teaching method.

Consider for a moment just how effective storytelling can be to communicate the truth of the Scriptures: it captivates the **attention** of the students, helps them to **understand** biblical truth, causes them to **remember** it, and helps them to **apply** it to their own lives! Can you name another method of teaching that is as effective?

Storytelling is a powerful, effective method of teaching, often used by the Son of God Himself. Frivolous? Hardly! Thanks for writing.

Your friend,

Andy

7.

PUTTING THE PERSUASIVE POWER OF PUPIL PARTICI- PATION INTO PRACTICE

"So how did your Children's Church go yesterday?" Larry asked early one Monday morning.

"It's going very well," Tim answered with a grin as he started an inventory on a parts tray. "Remember the extra row of chairs? Well, we had to use some of them yesterday! We had thirty-eight kids!"

"Fantastic!" Larry exulted. "Your group is growing!"

"Oh yes. The kids are responding very well, and we're enjoying working with them. We've had several saved, and now we're starting to get some positive comments from parents."

"That's always good. How's your discipline in class?"

"It's improved *tremendously*," Tim replied with enthusiasm. "We've implemented a lot of your ideas, and they're working well. There's still an occasional problem, of course, but they're few and far between now." He paused, and then continued, "There is one thing that I've been wanting to ask you, though."

"What's that?"

"We have a few kids that don't participate in anything," Tim told him, glancing up from the parts tray. "Not many, maybe just two or three. But they won't sing, won't work on the memory verse with us, won't do anything. They just sit there, and it kinda bothers me."

"That would bother me too," Larry replied. "You need to draw those kids out of their shells and get them involved. Pupil participation is vital. Are you using Bible games?"

Tim shrugged. "You loaned us that one game, and we used it the first Sunday. The kids loved it! But I thought you wanted it back, so we didn't use it after that first time."

"Use the review games every week," Larry suggested. "In two or three weeks, even your most reticent kids will be participating! Then they usually get involved in the other parts of the program as well.

"There are a number of ways you can get the kids participating. By increasing student involvement you enhance the teaching situation and minimize discipline problems. It's rewarding to teach when you and the students both enjoy class together. Pupil participation can add some zip and sparkle to class time."

> **Active participation holds student interest and leads to order and good behavior.**

As usual, Larry is right on target with his advice to Tim. Pupil participation makes learning fun, exciting and enjoyable, both for the teacher and the pupils. Active participation holds student interest at its keenest and leads to order and good behavior. Work to develop ways to involve your students in the teaching process, and they'll hurry into class, eager to participate and learn.

Your teaching hour offers myriad opportunities to bring the boys and girls into the program. In any class setting, participation is better than presentation. It is more interesting for them to **do** than to watch or listen. The wise teacher will seek out every opportunity to get the pupils involved. Controlled activity through pupil participation

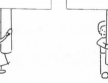

KIDS love to HELP!

Get us involved!

will contribute much to their interest and attention.

Here are some ways to get your kids involved in the ministry of your teaching hour:

1. **Use them as volunteers for various class duties.** Kids love to help, so why not let them? Use your students as helpers during the program, and they'll love you for it! You can actually present it as a special privilege and use it as a behavior incentive: "I need four quiet volunteers to help hold the visuals for the next song. Let's see who's sitting up straight and quiet."

So go ahead and assign those special jobs, basing the selection, if you wish, on behavior. Use your students to:

    a. Usher (take the offering)
    b. Hold visualized songs
    c. Assist with object lessons
    d. Pass out materials before, during, or after class
    e. Ring the bell for the Bible game
    f. Run projectors or video players (with proper supervision)
    g. Lead in prayer
    h. Take reports to church office
    i. Obtain supplies or equipment from office
    j. Even erase the boards or pack visuals after class!

Try to involve as many different children as possible in the various jobs, being careful to avoid choosing the same kids repeatedly to the exclusion of others. One director of a children's ministry continuously favored his granddaughter over the other students, resulting in the other kids' resenting the girl! Do your best to remember from week to week which pupils have been selected. Be sensitive to the complaint, "I never get chosen." It's often legitimate!

2. **Make use of Sword drills.** A "Sword drill" is simply an exercise in finding Scripture passages quickly. It helps acquaint the students with the layout of their Bibles and helps them learn to find passages.

A Sword drill is usually conducted this way: Give the order, "Draw Swords," and each student holds his closed Bible overhead with one hand. Announce the Scripture reference twice: "II Peter 3:18. II Peter

3:18. Charge!" At the command, "Charge!" the students begin searching for the passage. The first child to find the passage then stands to his feet with his finger on the verse. The teacher recognizes the first to stand and tells the child to read the verse. If the student cannot begin reading immediately, it becomes obvious that he did not have the verse ready when he stood, and another student is chosen.

Conduct the Sword drill with team competition (boys against girls, third grade against fourth, etc.) and give one point to the team of the child finding the verse. Then ask a question from the verse, and give a second point to the student who answers it. The class will quiet immediately and listen as the verse is read, knowing that a question is to follow.

As you plan your Sword drill, be sure to select verses that tie in with the day's lesson. Thus the Sword drill gives practice in finding Scripture passages and reinforces the truths of the lesson. Sword drills provide an excellent method of student participation, but keep them brief, and don't plan one every week.

3. **Use Scripture puzzles.** On the chalkboard, marker board or overhead projection transparency, draw the appropriate number of blanks for a brief, key phrase from Scripture, such as "Seek ye first the kingdom of God," or "But be ye doers of the word," or "Serve him in truth with all your heart," etc. Beneath the blanks draw a score box on one side and a bomb with an extremely long fuse on the other.

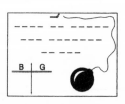
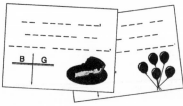

The puzzle is played hangman-style. Alternate between the two teams, allowing students to guess letters in the puzzle and filling in the correct letters guessed. Give one point for each letter as it appears in the phrase. If a letter is guessed that does not appear in the phrase, light the fuse on the bomb, allowing it to burn even further for each incorrect guess. If the bomb goes off, both teams lose and the teacher wins.

(My book, *Let's Play a Bible Game!* published by Meriwether Publishing, contains transparency masters for thirty-two different Scripture puzzles. Each verse, of course, is from the King James Version.)

4. **Teach with the question-and-answer method.** Another powerful teaching method that Jesus used quite frequently is the question-and-answer method. This method is invaluable to the teacher in that it encourages pupil participation, focuses attention on the truths of the lesson, stimulates the pupils to think, and provides the teacher with a means for evaluating student comprehension.

As you teach the lesson, ask appropriate, well-planned questions. The objective of these questions is to focus student attention on the lesson and get the students deeply involved in the learning process.

The question & answer method
1. **Elicits pupil participation.**
2. **Focuses attention on the lesson.**
3. **Sets the pupil to thinking.**
4. **Provides the teacher with feedback.**

Your questions should be of two basic types. The first is the thought question, which requires some thinking on the part of your kids: "Why did God say that King Ahab was more wicked than all the kings before him?" When you ask a thought question, eliminate the possibility of students' just blurting out an answer by prefacing your question with the words, "Raise your hand if you know." You would say, "Raise your hand if you know, Why did God say that King Ahab...?"

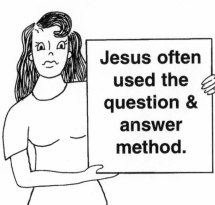

Jesus often used the question & answer method.

The second type of question is simply for emphasis or repetition, and differs from the thought question in form and in the manner in which it is presented. For instance, as you present the plan of salvation and the cross you might ask, "What happened three days and three nights after Jesus died?"

You want the entire class to respond aloud, so indicate this by asking the question, then cupping your hand behind your ear and saying, "Just tell me." Before long, your students will recognize that you desire a verbal response when you simply cup your hand behind your ear as you phrase the question.

Make much use of the question-and-answer method. It's very effective in that it elicits pupil **participation**, focuses **attention** on the lesson, sets the pupil to **thinking**, and provides you with a barometer of student **comprehension**. It's no wonder that Jesus often used the question-and-answer method.

5. **Have students read Scriptures in unison**. Rather than read Scripture passages to your students, encourage pupil participation and involvement by having them read the Bible verses aloud with you. The Word of God often makes a deeper impression when the students read it aloud, rather than simply hearing it read.

The teacher who has his students read in unison will face two obstacles: many times class members will have the inferior, modern translations (which can create confusion); also, time is lost, and interest wanders when some of the slower pupils take too long finding the passages.

Eliminate both of these problems by visualizing the Scripture verses on large flashcards or overhead projector transparencies! The overhead transparencies in particular are very easy to prepare if you are using a number of Scripture verses. It's a cinch to prepare professional-quality transparencies on your computer, using your printer or photocopier to make each transparency. Remember, each verse should be on a separate transparency. If you have access to a color printer, use it to highlight key words or phrases in the verse by printing them in another color!

And that he died for all, that they which live should not henceforth live unto themselves, but unto him which died for them, and rose again.

II Corinthians 5:15

Display the verse on the flashcard or overhead as you say, "Read II Corinthians 5:15 with me." Give the signal to begin reading by saying, "Reading...," or "Together..."

Read the reference first, then the text, then the reference again.

6. **Have students repeat key phrases.** As you prepare your lesson, watch for a key phrase that emphasizes the aim or thrust of the lesson. Have the students repeat it at various points throughout the lesson.

For example, when teaching the story of Noah, I emphasize the folly of the unbelievers by repeating the statement, "They didn't believe Noah, and they didn't believe God." At eight or ten different points in the story I repeat the statement for emphasis. From about the third time and following, the entire group says it with me each time.

When preaching on I Samuel 12:24, I repeatedly emphasize the phrase, "with all your heart." At various points during the Bible message I'll ask, "How does God want you to serve Him?" Back comes the answer, "With all your heart!"

This simple technique can be used to focus the attention of the students directly on the heart of your lesson. It helps keep their attention and deepens the impact of your teaching.

7. **Use the role-play method.** This is a teaching method that can be a lot of fun. It provides opportunity for student participation and, when properly used, captures and holds the attention of every student.

"The attention of my students is at its keenest on the occasions that we use role-playing!"

Let's say that you're teaching on Ephesians 4:32. During the presentation of your lesson, call two students to the front of the class and have them role-play a situation to illustrate a kind, forgiving spirit. Instruct the two volunteers to pretend that they are brother and sister. The sister has just done something unkind and mean-spirited to her brother (name something specific—maybe she intentionally switched off the computer to erase a game of her brother's), and now the brother must decide how he will respond.

Why did you turn off the computer?

You might even have them role-play the situation twice—the first time as the brother would probably want to respond in the flesh, and the second, as Christ would have him respond based on Ephesians 4:32.

On occasion, you might even tell the first part of a Bible story to establish the situation, then allow various students to role-play the part of some of the Bible characters! Let them decide for themselves how the person in question might have, or should have, responded. This will bring that Bible story to life, especially for those involved in the role-play. Before concluding the message, of course, finish the story according to the biblical record.

Role-playing can be a lot of fun, and the interest factor of this teaching method is tremendous! You'll not use it every week, of course, but it's very effective when used occasionally.

8. **Review your lesson with Bible games**. This exciting teaching method is the epitome of student participation! A Bible game is a fantastic way to review the lesson and reemphasize the key points. Bible games deepen the impression made by an effective lesson, and they give you an unparalleled opportunity to correct wrong ideas that your students may hold. If your students don't get involved in the Bible game, they're not going to get involved in anything!

Try this simple Bible game known as "Bombs Away!" Cut thirty-eight 3" squares from colored poster board or card stock. Place numerals from 1 to 10 on thirty of the cards (three of each numeral) and draw a bomb on each of the eight remaining cards. Scatter the thirty-eight game cards facedown on a table or lectern.

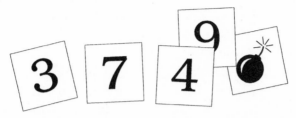

To play the game, simply ask review questions from the day's Bible lesson. When a student correctly answers a question, have him or her come forward and select a card. The number on the card represents the points scored for that student's team. The student may continue selecting cards and scoring points for as long as he desires; but if he finds a bomb, his turn ends, and he loses all the points from his turn!

Here's an interesting variation: make two or three cards with two bombs on each. When a student finds a double bomb, his turn ends, and he loses the points from his turn to the other team!

Or try the old scissors-paper-rock game. Cut thirty-six 3" squares from two different colors of card stock or poster board. Draw a rock on six cards of each color, a pair of scissors on six cards of each color, and paper on the remaining six of each color. Scatter the cards facedown in two separate groups, designating one color for each team.

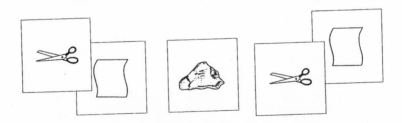

The student correctly answering the question comes forward and selects a card from his team's pile, then one from the opposing team's. As you know, scissors win over paper, paper over rock, and rock over scissors. Both cards go to the team that wins out. In the event of a tie (say the student draws two rocks), two more cards are drawn, with all four cards going to the winner. At the conclusion of the game, each card scores 1,000 points for the team possessing it.

Either of the above games may be made on felt squares and played on the flannel board for greater visibility, or make them on circles and draw them from a grab bag for use on the bus! (Circles come out of the grab bag easier than squares.)

(My book, *Teaching with Bible Games*, contains patterns and instructions for twenty Bible games for use on the flannel board. Another one of my books, *Let's Play a Bible Game!* contains instructions and transparency masters for sixteen overhead projector Bible games as well as transparency masters for thirty-two hangman-type Scripture puzzles. Both books are published by Meriwether Publishing and are available through your local Christian bookstore or directly from the publisher.

My two newest books, *Overhead Projector Games* and *More! Overhead Projector Games*, each contain seven different, ready-made transparency Bible games on attractive, two-color transparencies. These two books are published by Standard Publishing and are available from the publisher or your local bookstore.)

Recommended Sword of the Lord Publishers book: *"I Can't Wait Till Sunday Morning!"* (nine additional games). Bible review games are fun and exciting for teachers and students alike. The games are an excellent way to review and evaluate your lessons. This enjoyable teaching method adds zip and sparkle to your teaching program and encourages the students to listen carefully to your lessons. Once you get started on Bible games, you'll find out just what student participation is all about!

9. Get your students involved in Scripture memorization.

Your Primaries and Juniors are at the ideal age for memorizing—it will never be easier than right now—and Bible memorization should be a part of your teaching ministry. Many teachers (both Sunday school and Children's Church) attempt to "assign" a different memory verse every week. Very few of the students actually learn the verses, and it's easy to become discouraged and give up on Scripture memory.

It's usually better to work on just one a month. If you teach, drill, recite and review one verse for four weeks straight, almost every student who has attended regularly will know it without even trying! It's far better to teach twelve new verses each year, and have your students really memorize and remember them, than it is to "teach" fifty-two

verses that no one recalls at the end of the year.

Introduce the new verse on the first Sunday of the month with a short drill (five to seven minutes). Before class begins, write the verse out on a dry erase board or overhead transparency, with the reference before and after the text. As you introduce the verse in class, read it aloud one time, explaining any new words or unfamiliar expressions.

Then have the entire class read the verse aloud several times, including the reference. After reading the verse two or three times in unison, have the boys stand and read the verse, then the girls, then those students wearing red, then those wearing green or yellow, then those who are Chicago Bulls fans, etc. The object is to have the class read the verse *aloud* several times.

After reading the verse aloud six or eight times, begin erasing one or two words each time the verse is read, continuing until the entire verse is erased. Allow the students to choose the words to be erased, but inform them that you are choosing only those students who are reading the verse each time. You'll usually get one hundred percent participation!

Drill the verse for just a few minutes each Sunday for the first three weeks. Keep the drills short and exciting, visualizing the verse in a different way each week (overhead projector, marker board, flannel board, chalkboard, etc.).

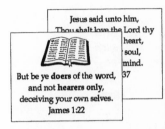

Hand out memory-verse tokens (small slips of paper with the verse attractively printed on them) as you dismiss at the end of the period. The next Sunday, give out a word search that uses every word in the verse. On the third Sunday have a printed verse puzzle or quiz to hand out, etc. Handouts can be very effective in memory work.

On the fourth Sunday of the month, review the verse very briefly, then allow the kids to recite it to receive a small prize.

I strongly suggest using only the King James Version for memory work. Children memorize it easily, the translation is accurate, and it gives a uniformity to your memory work as a class. The Word of God has been under attack throughout history, but in recent years the battle has intensified. More and more churches are giving in and going to other versions, resulting in confusion and division. Why not stay with the King James?

Periodically review the previous verses for the year. Display them on bulletin boards or verse cards on the walls, plan special memory contests, and occasionally review them in your Bible games. Your Primaries and Juniors are fantastic memorizers, and that skill should be directed toward the Word!

Encouraging Bible Memorization:

1. **Teach one verse each month.**
2. **Visualize the verse.**
3. **Drill each Sunday.**
4. **Use memory-verse tokens.**
5. **Have a monthly contest.**
6. **Use the King James Version.**
7. **Review previous verses.**
8. **Memorize along with the students.**

"So how about loaning me that Bible game book I saw over at your house?" Tim asked as he and Larry headed for the time clock to punch out. "What's it called—something about teaching with Bible games?"

"That's it," Larry replied, "*Teaching with Bible Games.* It's by a children's evangelist named Ed Dunlop, and it has some really awesome review games in it! We try to plan a tremendous amount of variety in our Children's Church program, but we use a Bible game almost every Sunday. They're that effective."

"Well, I'm gonna plan to use some of the other pupil participation stuff we talked about today, but I really need to get started using Bible games on a regular basis. If you'll loan me the book, Lisa and I will get started making some of our own games this week."

"You've got it!" Larry promised as he shoved his time card into the slot at the base of the clock. "I'll bring it to work tomorrow. I'm glad you're serious about using the games—they'll bring your program to life! You won't believe how excited your students will become about your class!"

Get your students participating!

1. Use them as volunteers in class.
2. Use Sword drills to reinforce the lesson.
3. Use Scripture puzzles.
4. Teach with the question & answer method.
5. Have students read Scripture in unison.
6. Have them repeat key phrases.
7. Use the role-play method.
8. Review your lesson with Bible games.
9. Involve your students in Scripture memory.

So, to be effective, you must...

Prepare.

Use visuals.

Reward good behavior.

Spruce up your classroom.

Teach with enthusiasm and excitement.

Captivate attention by using relevant stories.

Get your students participating in the program.

Pupil Participation

1. Name 8 class duties in which you can use student volunteers:
   (a)
   (b)
   (c)
   (d)
   (e)
   (f)
   (g)
   (h)

2. Name 6 teaching methods that utilize student participation and thereby captivate attention:
   (a)
   (b)
   (c)
   (d)
   (e)
   (f)

3. How do you get the rest of the class to listen when one student reads the verse during a Sword drill?

4. How can you use a Sword drill to reinforce the day's lesson?

5. What Master Teacher made extensive use of the question-and-answer method?

6. How do you prevent students from blurting out an answer before you call on one specific student?

7. What two obstacles to reading in unison does the teacher overcome by visualizing the Scripture verses on overhead transparencies or flashcards?

8. Give two reasons why role-playing is an effective teaching method when used occasionally:
   (a)
   (b)

Bible Game Checklist

YES NO

___ ___   1. Do I fully understand the reasons for using Bible review games?

___ ___   2. Am I using this Bible game as a teaching tool to review, apply and reinforce the lesson?

___ ___   3. Are my review questions written out?

___ ___   4. Are they clear and concise?

___ ___   5. Do they cover the main points of the lesson?

___ ___   6. Did I avoid "trick" questions?

___ ___   7. Do I have a combination of Bible fact and Bible application questions?

___ ___   8. Do I fully understand the rules for this game so that I can explain it simply to my students?

___ ___   9. Are the game pieces in the game folder?

___ ___   10. Does my "game spotter" understand the need to choose students from all parts of the classroom and to select evenly from both teams?

___ ___   11. Am I prepared to conduct the Bible game with excitement, yet maintain classroom control at all times?

___ ___   12. Do I plan to set up the game before class so my students will not have to wait?

           13. When was the last time I used this game in class?

___ ___   14. Do I keep a written record?

___ ___   15. Do I use a VARIETY of games so they are always fresh and exciting?

144

Ask Andy!

Dear Andy,

We visualize a lot of Scripture verses on the overhead projector and have the students read them aloud during the lesson, but I've noticed that the kids stumble over the reference when we abbreviate the name of the book. Should we take the time to teach our kids the abbreviations to the books of the Bible?

Dustin D. Furniture

Dear Dustin,

A far simpler solution would be to write out the name of the book for each reference. Abbreviating the reference doesn't save that much time, and seems to lead to confusion, as you found out.

Even when working with adults, I stay away from abbreviating the books of the Bible.

Andy

Dear Andy,

Which is easier to read: capital lettering or lower case? (We've been arguing about it in the last couple of teachers' meetings.)

Sandy Hill

Dear Sandy,

Lower-case lettering is always easier to read, and that's important when you're teaching Primaries who are just learning to read. Don't do any of your visuals in all caps.

For the children,

Andy

Dear Andy,

We use Bible games in Master Clubs, and we love them! The games are an excellent way to review, and student participation is excellent. The problem is that many of our students get rowdy and noisy during the games.

We really enjoy the games and recognize that they are a dynamic teaching method, but we can't put up with the noise and disorder that sometimes result. What should we do?

Star Gazer

Dear Star,

Bible games are exciting and a lot of fun, and your students will enjoy them thoroughly. They're a really effective way to review, but some students will take advantage of the relaxed atmosphere during the game if you let them. Don't let them!

Next week when you announce your Bible game, remind the class that only students who are quiet and orderly will be called on to answer questions. If a particular student becomes noisy or disruptive, have a worker remove him/her to the back of the room.

When you deal swiftly with problem behavior, the class will quickly learn that they can get excited and have fun but must stay within your boundaries.

Enjoy the games!

Andy

8.
THE VERIFIABLE VALUE
OF VISITATION

Tim slowed the Lexus and turned into a narrow, rutted lane. Tall oaks grew on each side of the roadway, their branches meeting overhead to form a dark green canopy. The undergrowth on both sides was a tangled mass of brambles and vines, and weeds grew waist-high in the center strip of road. The lane was dark, almost spooky.

"Feels like we're in the African jungle, doesn't it?" Lisa whispered.

Tim nodded. "Jason's bus captain warned us that this is a rough home situation, but I never imagined that he lived in a place like this." He steered around a mudhole. "By the way, what grade is Jason in?"

Lisa frowned. "Sixth, I think."

They drove into a clearing and climbed from the car. Both gazed at the scene before them and instantly felt sorry for Jason. The house was hardly more than a shed, with a poorly patched roof and a sagging porch. Trash was piled everywhere: old rusting cars, refrigerators, tires, and odds and ends of lumber. Beer cans and whiskey bottles were scattered here and there among the waist-high weeds.

A heavy woman sprawled on a dilapidated couch on the porch, an opened beer can beside her. She was wearing the biggest pair of worn-out blue jeans Tim had ever seen, and her shirt, half-buttoned, looked as though it hadn't been washed in two weeks. Tim could tell she was drunk. His stomach tightened in fear as he and Lisa walked toward the porch.

The woman half opened her eyes and saw them standing timidly at the edge of the cinder-block steps. "Who are you?" The words came out in a snarl.

Tim found his voice. "Mrs. Lewis? I'm Tim Wellington, and this—"

"What do you want?" She wasn't even giving Tim a chance to answer the original question.

"We came out to visit you and Jason." In surprise, Lisa realized that the second voice was her own. "We want you to know that we enjoy having Jason—"

"Git off my property!" Tim and Lisa stood stunned, and she repeated the command. "I said git off! Now!"

The door opened, and Jason appeared on the porch. Embarrassment was written all over his face. "Ma," he began, "these are my teachers from church. This is Mr. and Mrs. Wellington. They're the best—"

The woman cursed and then said, "I want them gone. Now!"

Jason gave the Wellingtons an embarrassed, apologetic look. "Ma, they just came out to talk to you."

The beefy woman cursed violently, this time leaping to her feet in a move that was amazing for someone her size. In a flash, she raised one heavy arm, then swung it sideways at Jason, striking him in the head. Jason was a big, muscular kid, but the blow knocked him off balance, causing him to strike his head against the door frame.

To Tim's horror, the woman was on her son in an instant, striking him on the head and shoulders. "Don't never talk back to me, boy!" she screeched. Finally, she shoved him sprawling through the open door.

She turned back to her visitors, and they hastily stepped backwards. "Are you leavin' or what?" Tim didn't need a second invitation.

Lisa was crying as the Lexus reached the end of Jason's driveway. "I didn't know!" she sobbed. "I just didn't know!"

Tim's face was hard, and his eyes were narrow slits. Lisa had never seen him so upset. "That's alcohol for you!" he stammered, so angry he could hardly get the words out. "That ungodly stuff destroys people! And that big woman is trying to relieve her frustrations by abusing Jason."

His expression suddenly softened as he turned to Lisa. "Jason really needs us, doesn't he? I'm beginning to understand why he acts the way he does in class. His defiance and disrespect are just a cover-up for the hurt he's feeling inside. He's looking for love.

"Lisa, I'm not sure just what to do, but I'm going to make an extra effort to reach out to that boy."

Prospect Card	Absentee Visit	Follow-Up Visit
Name _____	Name _____	Name _____
Address _____	Address _____	Address _____
Phone _____	Phone _____	Phone _____
Age ____Class ____	Age ____Class ____	Age ____Class ____
Church_____	Last Date Attended ____	Decision _____
Comments: _____	Contacts Made: ____	_____Date ____

Class visitation is a vital part of any ministry, and this is especially true of a ministry to children. The teacher who desires to reach the heart of his students and win them to Christ, then teach and disciple them, must be willing to visit his kids in their homes. A teacher who neglects this aspect of his ministry cannot really expect to make a lasting impact upon the lives of his students.

Visitation serves a number of purposes. It shows the student and his parents that you care enough to go out of your way to make a visit to the home. It opens your eyes to the background, needs and makeup of the student—you get to know him. It also helps the student get to know you, seeing you perhaps for the first time as a real human being who cares about him, not just a talking head that shares Bible lessons on Sunday.

Visitation is vital to your ministry!

The teacher who cares VISITS!

The Lexus purred as it slowly made its way up the steep gravel drive. Tim steered hard to the right, trying to avoid the deep ruts in the roadway; but one wheel dropped into a rut, and the car bounced hard, dragging the underbody with a dreadful scraping sound. "I think we'll walk up next time," Tim remarked.

Lisa pointed. "There it is. Jake said it's the third trailer on the left."

The little cluster of mobile homes perched on the side of the hill in such a haphazard arrangement that one got the impression they were never meant to be there permanently. Trash littered most of the yards, and nearly every trailer showed signs of neglect and decay. Dogs were everywhere. Rock music assaulted the Wellingtons as they stepped from the car.

They hurried toward the single-wide, blue-and-white unit with the sagging deck, keenly aware of the hostile stares of three pot-smoking teenagers sitting on the hood of a junked car across the driveway. "Church people!" a thin, acne-faced girl sneered.

Nine-year-old Tina answered the door at Tim's knock. She took one look, then threw open the battered screen door to greet them both with delighted hugs. "Mom!" she screeched. "It's my teachers!" Lisa was conscious of the snickers from the teenagers.

A thin man in shorts and a ragged undershirt came to the door with a cigarette in his hand. He coldly looked at Tim and Lisa, blew a cloud of smoke in their direction, then started to turn away.

"Ah...I'm Tim Wellington," Tim stammered. "Are you Tina's dad?"

The man turned and sarcastically snorted. "I guess not, pal. I'm...just a friend of her mother's. Somethin' I can do for you?"

"This is David," Tina volunteered. "He's my mom's new boyfriend."

"David, I'm Tim Wellington, and this is my wife, Lisa," Tim said warmly, extending his hand. David shook it reluctantly. "We teach the Children's Church at Calvary Baptist Church, and Tina is one of our students."

David just nodded.

"We wanted to visit Tina," Tim continued, "and let her and you know that we enjoy having her in class. She's a sweet girl."

David reached out a dirty hand and flipped one of Tina's braids. "He doesn't know you, does he, kid?"

"Anyway, we'd like to invite you to come visit us," Tim said, reaching into his pocket and handing David a gospel tract with the Calvary Baptist imprint on the front. "I think you'd enjoy the services, and you'd meet a lot of friendly people."

David looked at the proffered tract but made no move to take it. "I'm not much on church," he muttered.

Tim smiled and continued to hold out the tract. "But come give us a try," he coaxed. "If you don't like it, you never have to come back."

The man closed the screen door between Tim and himself. "I told you I ain't got no time for church. Now, don't push it, mister. Tina can go if she wants, but leave me alone, or I'll decide that she can't go neither." With that, he turned and disappeared into the gloom of the trailer.

Tina pushed past them to open the screen door. "I'll go find my mom," she offered.

She was back quickly. "Mom says she's busy."

Lisa hugged her. "Well, we came to see you, Tina," she told the girl. "We want you to know that we're glad you're in our Children's Church."

"Well, I'm glad you and Mr. Tim are my teachers," Tina responded. "You're the best! And you know something? You're the only teachers who come to see me. Mr. Jake, my bus captain, comes to see me every Saturday, but the other teachers never do!"

They stood and talked with Tina for a few more minutes, then headed down the walk. Tina ran after them and gave them each a hug as they climbed into the car.

"She's a real sweetheart, isn't she?" Lisa remarked as Tim started the car. "But what a home situation!"

Tim was deep in thought as he turned the Lexus around, then rolled slowly toward the steep driveway. He glanced over just in time to see one of the teenagers flick a cigarette butt at the Lexus, bouncing it off the windshield. The thin-faced girl hopped off the car, then turned toward them with an action so vile and lewd that Tim turned away in embarrassment and disgust.

* * *

"So you're the Wellingtons," the tall, good-looking man said, extending a hand to Tim and then to Lisa. "Pleased to meet you. The twins talk about you constantly."

"Mr. Bradford, we enjoy having Dana and David in class," Tim replied. "We just wanted to stop by and meet you and tell the twins that we're glad they're a part of our Children's Church."

"Forgive me for not inviting you in," Mr. Bradford said as he took a step backwards and leaned against the porch railing. "The twins are out shopping with their mother, and I'm leaving for an appointment in just a few minutes."

"That's okay," Tim replied. "Hey, we won't keep you, but let me just give you this and invite you and Mrs. Bradford to come visit us."

The man took the tract and looked it over, then tucked it in his shirt pocket. "Thanks, Tim. We just might do that sometime."

Tim turned toward the steps. "Well, thanks for your time. Please tell the twins we're sorry we missed them. And don't forget our invitation. We'd really love to have you."

Mr. Bradford laid a hand on Tim's arm. "Before you go, I want to say thank you for teaching David and Dana. I know they're a handful sometimes, but we want you to know that we appreciate you working with them. They talk about you two constantly. 'Mr. Wellington says this. Mr. Wellington told us that.'"

He suddenly laughed. "To be honest, I guess we were expecting a couple of super-heroes, the way the twins talk about you. My kids love you."

He held out a hand to Tim. "Hey, thanks again for stopping by. I'm sorry, but I've gotta run. But I want you to know that Donna and I appreciate what you're doing with our kids. We'll take you up on the invitation to visit your church sometime."

Tim and Lisa walked toward the car. "Well, that was encouraging," Tim remarked. "A little better than the last two visits, anyway."

Visitation does not enhance your ministry; it's part of your ministry.

The teacher who visits in the homes of his students gets to know them and is therefore better prepared to meet their needs.

The teacher who visits shows his students and their families that he really cares.

The teacher who visits has opportunities to minister to the parents and other family members of his students and is sometimes rewarded by seeing them get saved and become a part of the church ministry.

The teacher who visits his students begins to form close relationships with them, greatly improving his knowledge of their needs and therefore enabling himself to minister more effectively.

Don't be shocked by the homelife of some of your students.

Visitation will sometimes break your heart. It's distressing to witness the homelife of some of the children. Some of those little children who sit before you on Sunday morning come from homes that expose them to pornography, drugs, alcohol, tobacco, witchcraft and Devil worship, rock music, incest and molestation, and every other evil that the depraved human mind can imagine. It's not unusual to walk away from a home feeling defiled by just having been there; but remember that some of "your kids" live in that environment day after day!

Don't allow the deplorable home situations of your students to drive you to discouragement and despair. Instead, allow these situations to drive you to your knees in prayer for your students!

Perhaps the greatest benefit from home visitation is what it can do for you as a teacher: it can give you a broken heart; and when the child of God teaches from a broken heart, his teaching takes on new depth and meaning.

Visitation will sometimes break your heart!

How long has it been since you've been in the home of every one of your students? How long has it been since you've taught

Welcome

through tears of compassion and concern for your students?

Set a goal to visit in the home of each of your students at least once a quarter. If you teach a large class, enlist some help with this important visitation project, and assign some of the visits to others, but follow up to be sure that the task is carried out.

Your visitation efforts will take several forms:

Absentee visitation is very important, and you'll want to be sure to make a visit as soon as you realize that one of your class members has started to miss class. Many of the students who dropped out of church and disappeared forever could have been reclaimed if a teacher had only cared enough to make a visit!

New prospect visitation is important, and any teacher who has a burden for souls and a zeal to build his class for the glory of God will be constantly on the lookout for ways to reach new children.

Do you teach with a broken heart?

Problem-solving visits are sometimes necessary to resolve conflicts between students or clear up misunderstandings that arise in class.

Perhaps the most time-consuming but most important are the visits to your **regulars**. It's vital to visit your students just to get to know them and therefore be equipped to meet their needs.

Each of your students is vastly different from every other student in class, and the needs of all are so varied! Some of your kids are confident and self-assured, while others are timid and fearful. Some are outgoing and friendly, while others are reserved and quiet. Some live for sports, while others are intimidated by athletic pursuits and want nothing to do with sports. Some come from godly, healthy homes where Christ is honored, while others are from abusive, oppressive homes where evil is glorified and the name of Christ is blasphemed.

You need to visit in the home of each of your students and get to know his or her individual needs. Imagine a doctor who would write you a prescription without having diagnosed your illness or even heard a description of your symptoms!

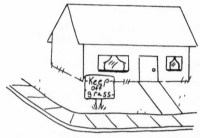

Here are some quick guidelines for effective children's ministry visitation:

Dress neatly, but casually. Unless you're visiting in a very affluent area, you'll usually be received better if you are not overdressed. Remember, you are representing both the name of Christ and your church, so avoid sloppiness.

Always be polite and courteous. Remember that in reality you are an uninvited trespasser. You're in the same situation as Esther when she ventured uninvited into the throne room, hoping to receive the welcome of an extended scepter. Sometimes your visit will be received with delight, sometimes with hostility and contempt. Even when you are treated rudely, remember that you represent the cause of Christ and don't be tempted to lash back with your own rudeness.

How many times I've received a rude welcome and been tempted to respond in kind, but by God's grace I've been able to remain polite and friendly and then been able to reach the family at a later date!

Be careful to use sidewalks rather than cutting across people's lawns. Respect "day-sleeper" signs. (But ignore the "no trespassing" and "no soliciting" ones; they're usually put up by timid people who have no

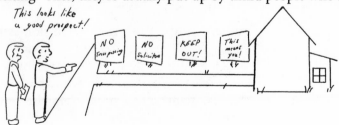

sales resistance.) Approach the house, mobile home or apartment with a smile on your face. Be warm, cheerful and friendly as you talk to people. Above all, be courteous!

Introduce yourself, your church and your children's ministry. Many times the people you visit are unfriendly and ill at ease until they find out who you are and what you are after. Take time to be friendly and make small talk, but get to the point quickly.

Use quality printed materials. Attractive church brochures and tracts help establish your credibility and provide the subject of your visit with valuable information about your church and ministry. Even when you get a cool reception, do your best to leave a gospel tract and church brochure before you leave. Many, many times we have reached hostile, unfriendly people in this way!

Keep your visit brief. Always remember that you were uninvited and don't overstay your welcome. If the people you are visiting are warm and friendly, and obviously sincere in their attempts to get you to stay longer, then take them up on it. If they are coolly polite, be alert enough to know when it is time to leave. Sometimes the shortest visits are the most effective ones.

Keep a file on each of your students. One of the primary purposes of home visitation is to get to know your students in order to minister to them most effectively. Why not keep a record of the information that you glean from your visitation—a card with data such as name, address, phone number, age and birthday, but also personal information such as hobbies, the name of his Little League team, likes and dislikes, dates of salvation, baptism, etc.?

Visit with a partner. Visitation can sometimes be discouraging if you go alone, so take a partner: your spouse, another teacher or worker, even some of the kids from your class! The task is much more enjoyable when you share it with a friend.

Visit during "key" time periods. Visiting deserted homes accomplishes absolutely nothing, so do a little research and find out what time of day families in your area are most likely to be at home. In our ministry at Calvary Baptist Church in Chattanooga, Tennessee, we found that the best time to visit was right after school, from three-thirty to five-thirty in the afternoon. During that time slot, we actually found about ninety percent of our kids at home!

When we conducted a Kids' Crusade in Dalton, Georgia, and visited during the same time period, we found almost no one home. To build a ministry in Dalton, one would have to find a more effective time to visit—perhaps later in the evening.

Schedules and lifestyles vary from one locale to the next, so try to schedule your visitation efforts during the days and times when you are most likely to find folks in your area at home.

"Let's do one more stop before we head for home," Lisa suggested. "I have a card here for Steven Holloway, 1714 Buena Vista Drive. I think that's close to here."

"Steven Holloway," Tim echoed. "Who's he?"

"He's the skinny, blond kid with the thick glasses who came once or twice when we first started teaching. I don't think he's been there for two or three weeks."

Tim shook his head. "I can't place him."

Moments later the Lexus rolled to a stop in front of an attractive split-level. A stocky man was washing a late-model pickup truck in the driveway.

"Calvary Baptist Church, huh?" Mr. Holloway said while glancing over the church brochure. "Yeah, Steven went there on your church bus a couple of times. But he didn't seem to want to go back, so I'm not gonna make him."

"May we see him for a moment?" Tim asked. "We'd like to talk with him."

The man hesitated. "Okay," he finally said, "but don't try to badger him into coming back. If he doesn't want to, he doesn't want to."

"Sure," Tim agreed.

"Steven! Someone here to see you!" Mr. Holloway shouted in the direction of the house, then went back to hosing down the truck.

A thin boy appeared at the edge of the garage door, stood uncertainly for a moment, then reluctantly came forward to stand beside his father.

"Steven, these people are from the church," Mr. Holloway said. "They want to know if you would like to go to church again."

Wordlessly, Steven shook his head.

His father shrugged and grinned apologetically. "I guess that answers it."

"Steven," Tim said, "could you tell us why you don't want to come? We'd love to have you back."

Mr. Holloway held up one hand. "No pressure."

Tim turned toward him. "Yes sir. But I'd at least like to know why he doesn't want to come."

"Son, is there a reason why you don't want to go to church with these people?"

"Didn't you like Children's Church?" Tim questioned. "We've just started teaching, and we have a lot to learn, but we're trying to have a good program that you'll enjoy. Didn't you enjoy the program?"

The boy nodded. "But I couldn't see."

His father leaned down to him. "Couldn't see what, Son?"

Steven's eyes looked huge behind the thick glasses. "I tried to get a seat on the front row, Dad. But the other kids took all the seats, and when I told the man, he just told me to sit on the back row. He said I should get there early if I want to sit in front."

Mr. Holloway turned to face the Wellingtons. "Steven's vision is...well...far from adequate. We're not looking for special treatment, but it seems that a student with a visual impairment could at least sit in front so he could see!"

Tim nodded. "What man did you talk with, Steven? What did he look like?"

"He was tall and skinny," the boy answered slowly. "And bald-headed."

"That's Mr. Anderson," Lisa said. "I'm sure he didn't mean to be unkind."

"Whoever it was, you'd think he could have shown a little concern," Mr. Holloway remarked. "Steven's not looking for sympathy, but he could have used a little help in this area."

Tim nodded. "I'm sorry it happened this way, sir. By the way, I'm Tim Wellington, and my wife and I just took over the Children's Church program a few weeks ago. I want you to know that this deeply concerns me, and I want to see what we can do to make it a good situation for your son."

He turned to Steven. "How about if we reserve you a special seat on the front row? I'm the teacher, and I can do it!"

"The other kids will laugh at me."

"Not if we have a special reason for your being there," Tim told him. "Suppose we give you some special job. Say, what if you keep score for the Bible games?"

"I'm good at math," the boy replied hopefully.

"Then it's settled! We can make you the official scorekeeper, with a permanent front row seat. We won't even mention your eyesight to the other kids."

The boy looked up at his father. "Can I go, Dad?"

Mr. Holloway put a hand on his son's shoulder, then turned to Tim. "Tell the bus driver to pick Steven up this Sunday, would you?"

"I'm glad we made that visit," Lisa remarked as the Lexus sped toward home. "We would have lost Steven for good if we hadn't stopped."

Steven Holloway was back in church the very next Sunday, in the front row seat that Tim reserved for him, but he didn't get to enjoy his new role as the official scorekeeper for the Bible game in Children's Church that week. While the Bible game was in progress, he was in a counseling room asking Jesus to be his Saviour!

Visitation is vital.

So, to be effective, you must...

Prepare.

Use visuals.

Reward good behavior.

Spruce up your classroom.

Teach with enthusiasm and excitement.

Captivate attention by using relevant stories.

Get your students participating in the program.

Get to know your students through home visitation.

Effective Class Visitation

1. Dress neatly, but casually.
2. Always be polite and courteous.
3. Introduce yourself, your church and your children's ministry.
4. Use quality printed materials.
5. Keep your visits brief.
6. Maintain a file on each of your students.
7. Visit with a partner.
8. Find the most effective visitation time.

Checking Up on Class Visitation

YES NO

___ ___ 1. Is visitation a regular part of my ministry?

___ ___ 2. Do I visit every week?

___ ___ 3. Do I enjoy visitation?

___ ___ 4. Do I know each of my students well enough to pray intelligently for them?

___ ___ 5. When a student starts missing class, do I make certain that he receives a visit from me?

___ ___ 6. Do I visit regularly for new prospects?

___ ___ 7. Do I visit my regulars to get to know them, meet their families, and show that I care?

___ ___ 8. Am I always polite and courteous on visitation?

___ ___ 9. Do I always carry gospel tracts and church brochures?

___ ___ 10. Do I try to keep my visits brief, unless the Lord leads otherwise?

___ ___ 11. Do I keep an up-to-date information file on each of my students?

___ ___ 12. Do I involve my students in visitation?

Prospect Card

Name _____

Address _____

Phone _____

Age ____ Class ____

Church _____

Comments: _____

Absentee Visit

Name _____

Address _____

Phone _____

Age ____ Class ____

Last Date Attended

Contacts Made: _____

Follow-Up Visit

Name _____

Address _____

Phone _____

Age ____ Class _____

Decision _____

_____ Date ____

Ask Andy!

Dear Andy,

I recognize the importance of home visitation, but I have a hard time doing it. I'm an introvert, and it's hard for me to walk up to someone's door and just start talking. I live with an overwhelming fear of rejection, and to be honest, visitation terrifies me. When I approach a door, my heart starts racing, my head pounds with fear, and I break out in a cold sweat.

I want to do the best I can in my ministry to my kids, and I do try to make visits, but it's the hardest thing I've ever done in my life. Can you help me?

Dusty Lane

Dear Dusty,

Visitation isn't easy for anyone, but for some of us, it can be a fearful experience. I face many of the same fears as you. A verse of Scripture that has helped me tremendously is II Timothy 1:7, "For God hath not given us the spirit of fear; but of power, and of love, and of a sound mind."

Another thing that helps is to carry a "gimmick" with you. I always carry a pocketful of balloons and make balloon sculptures for the kids (and their parents) when I visit. I also use a trick nickel that squirts water right in the face of anyone who examines it closely! A youth director I know always carries two or three pocket magic tricks.

Learn to use some unusual item that will get the attention of the folks you visit and, especially, get them laughing with you. This sets everyone at ease and makes the visit a pleasant experience for everyone involved.

For the kids,

Andy

Dear Andy,

I've just started using the dry erase board, and I really like it. It's simple, easy to use, and extremely versatile. My question is this: How can I write or draw on the board so that my body is not blocking the board as I am writing? I've noticed that every time I use the board, my students are leaning out of their seats trying to see around me.

Amber Waves

Dear Amber,

If you are right-handed, your marker board should be to your left as you face your students. (As you turn to write on the board, it will then be on your right.) Simply stand at the end of the board (as close to the wall as possible) as you write. In this way the marker board will be visible to most of your class as you write or sketch.

For the kids,

Andy

9.
REAPING RICH RELATIONSHIPS

"Look at me!" four-year-old Ricky shouted as the bus bounced along our route. I glanced over in dismay to see him standing on the back of one of the bus seats! With a whoop of delight he did a perfect backflip to land in the next seat. I hurried back to grab him, but he was fast enough to scramble atop the seat and execute another perfect flip before I could reach him.

"Ricky, you've got to stay in your seat!" I fumed, grabbing him and carrying him forward. "Now stay there!" I slammed him into the seat just a little harder than was necessary.

"Let go of me!" he squealed, struggling to free himself from my grip. "Let go of me!"

"Ricky," I said through clenched teeth, "you've got to stay in your seat. You can't run all over the bus. You're gonna get hurt. Now stay there!"

"Let go of me!"

It was the same thing every week. Here I was, a Bible college student, engaging in a battle of wits with a four-year-old—and the four-year-old was winning! It was impossible to keep that kid in a seat. This was my first experience with the bus ministry, and nobody had ever told me that you weren't allowed to spank the bus kids, so...well, you figure it out.

I remember one time when the bus was doing about twenty miles an hour down a residential street. Ricky actually tried to leap out the window! Thankfully, I was able to catch him by the legs and haul him back in.

To be honest, I resented that kid. I saw him as an undisciplined brat who had never learned to obey. What a nuisance! Each Sunday I dreaded the moment that he would get on the bus, and looked forward to the moment he bounced off.

But then one day I learned that little daredevil Ricky was going blind. The doctors were not even sure just how much eyesight he had, but they told his parents that he would undoubtedly be totally blind before his fifth birthday.

I was devastated! Here was a little boy living in a dark, scary world that was growing darker every day. Suddenly every bit of resentment I had ever felt against that little guy was gone. How could I have ever treated a child so harshly? God used the news of Ricky's deteriorating eyesight and impending blindness to break my heart.

The next Sunday, as Ricky got on the bus, I called him to me. At that moment I realized that my bitterness and resentment had been replaced by the love of God. I actually loved this little acrobat! I hugged him tight. "Ricky, would you sit with me?" I invited, and to my relief, he did.

A special relationship began to form that day. To my amazement, I no longer had any trouble keeping Ricky in a seat. Instead of resenting him, I was learning to love him, and he saw the difference.

Kids will listen to a teacher who loves them!

God used that little guy to teach me a valuable lesson and set the direction for my ministry. No matter how rude or obnoxious the children may be, there's never any need to be harsh or hateful with them. We must be firm but gentle with them, and they need to see the love of Christ in us.

The teacher who truly cares for his students and wants to see them saved and living for Christ will do everything he can to develop special relationships with his students. He'll spend time with them. He'll get to know them and learn to love them. The teacher who cares enough to build those relationships with "his kids" will find that the effectiveness of his ministry to them is greatly increased.

LOVE

"Lisa and I have been visiting our kids," Tim told Larry as he struggled to loosen a troublesome bolt. **"We've both been horrified by the home situations we've found."**

He looked up from the workbench with tears in his eyes. "Larry, more than eighty percent of my bus kids are from broken homes! One of my third graders told me that she's had five different daddies. Divorce has devastated a lot of our church families too."

Larry nodded soberly. "It's a wicked world, Tim."

"But the homes these kids live in! One of my boys now lives in a foster home because he was molested by his mother, and *then* his grandmother! He doesn't even remember his father. Some of my kids come from homes where they see drugs and alcohol and pornography and immorality and..." Tim was sobbing so hard he couldn't continue.

Larry stepped over and put a hand on his shoulder. "Your kids need you, Tim. That's why God called you to teach Children's Church. It's an opportunity for you to show them the love of Jesus! Get close to them. Work to develop loving relationships with them. Spend time with them, pray for them, and show them that you care."

Tim nodded. "The first Sunday Lisa and I were in Children's Church I saw the kids as little monsters. To be honest, I almost hated them. It frustrated me to see them disobey and talk back and act so rude and disrespectful. It made me want to slap them up side the head, but now, Lisa and I love them. We want God to use us to reach them for Him. It hurts to see how much they want to please and do what's right, then remember the horrible situations they go home to every night."

"Don't let their homes get you down and discouraged," Larry said softly. "Instead, allow God to use your concern for them to motivate you to give your very best to your ministry, to challenge you to pray for them, and to show them the love of Christ. Spend time with your students, Tim. Show them you care. When you do, many of the behavior problems will disappear. Kids will listen to a teacher who loves them."

LOVE YOUR STUDENTS

Are you willing to spend the time it takes to develop close relationships with your students? How well do you know your pupils? How well do they know you? Do you really love your kids, and does it show? As Larry told Tim, "Kids will listen to a teacher who loves them."

Here are a few ways to develop a loving, caring relationship with the students in your class:

Hello, Michael!

1. **Learn each child's name, and use it often.** I've been appalled and dismayed at the number of teachers I meet who don't even know their students by name! That might be excusable if you teach a large group of two or three hundred and have a rapid turnover of students; but if you teach a class of thirty or forty or fifty, there's no reason at all why you should not be able to learn each and every child's name—unless, of course, you simply don't care.

2. **Listen when your students talk.** Be available before and after class, and pay close attention when your kids want to talk to you. Many times teachers are busy chatting with other teachers, and the kids don't have a chance to catch the teacher's attention. When you take the  time to listen to a child, that tells him that he's important to you.

3. **Visit in the home.** We just spent an entire chapter on this topic, but allow me to say this: I have never met a teacher who had a close, loving relationship with his students but did not visit them. The two go together.

4. **Plan outings for your class.** When you take the time to plan an

outing for your class, it tells your students in a tangible way that you love them; you want to be with them; you enjoy their company. Class outings help you build a close relationship with each student.

Imagine each child in your class as an island. As a teacher, you desire to take the Good News of Jesus and salvation to each island, and then the elements of growth and victory. You need to build a bridge of love, trust and understanding to each island in order to take the message over. The only way to build these bridges to your students is to spend time with them. One of the most effective ways to do this is to plan outings—times of fun and fellowship with your kids.

CLASS OUTINGS
establish rapport &
build relationships.

Class outings take time, planning and work, but they're worth every ounce of effort in the relationships that flourish as a result! How sad that believers today will commit themselves to Little League and scouting and civic causes, but are unwilling to commit themselves wholeheartedly to ministry in the local church!

For seven and a half years I served as assistant pastor and Christian education director at Calvary Independent Baptist Church in Chattanooga, Tennessee. Of all my ministries and duties at the church, the one I enjoyed most was our Children's Church.

Chattanooga is filled with churches, and many of them have bus ministries. It was difficult to develop faithfulness among our bus riders since there were so many churches to choose from and so many unethical bus captains always willing to draw kids away from another fundamental church.

We used outings to develop faithfulness and a loyalty to our church. My workers and I worked overtime to develop close relationships with our students, to demonstrate the love of Christ to them, and to meet their needs. We found that our kids especially enjoyed outdoor activities: cave trips, hikes, picnics and canoe trips. Our ministry to the children thrived and grew because our workers proved their love to the kids by spending time with them.

We planned an activity at least once a month, and we let the students help decide what types of activities to plan. Our workers became very close to our kids.

I suppose that the one event that was most effective in developing loyalty and faithfulness was our "overnights." Every six or eight weeks we had well over a hundred Primaries and Juniors spend the night at the church. The overnight started at six o'clock Friday evening and concluded at ten Saturday morning. Believe it or not, we always felt that the time was too brief!

We started the activity by dividing the group into six teams. An hour of relay races and active games gave the students the opportunity to score points for their teams. Then the teams went to separate classrooms for Bible studies with their team leaders. We even gave points for filling in the Bible study sheet. Students could gain points for their team by lining up quickly, displaying a cooperative attitude, and being quiet at the appropriate times, or lose points for disruptive behavior. On Saturday morning before dismissal, we gave a blue ribbon to each first-place team member, red ribbons to the second-place kids, and white for third. Half of the group went home with ribbons!

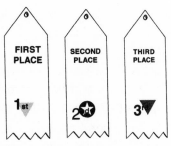

We planned a preaching service Friday evening, and another one on Saturday after breakfast. We actually had more teaching time during an overnight than we did on Sunday morning with Sunday school and Children's Church combined!

The highlight of the evening was the McDonald's trip. All the children brought their own money (which they turned in to the "bank" when they registered at the beginning of the overnight; the money was sealed in an envelope with each child's name on it, then returned to him or her just before we got to McDonald's). We took two buses (each to a *separate* location) and always called McDonald's a few days in advance to let them know we were coming. We planned to arrive at the restaurant about eleven o'clock, so we usually had the place to ourselves.

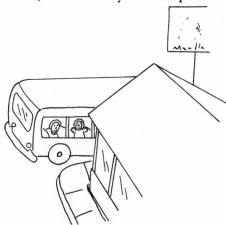

We returned from McDonald's just before midnight, then sang a few quiet songs together to settle the kids and get them ready for bed. The girls and lady workers slept upstairs in our Children's Church room, and the men and boys slept in two large classrooms downstairs, with bathroom facilities totally separate. We insisted that the kids get quiet and sleep; those who tried other ideas were excluded from the following overnight.

Everyone got up at seven-thirty. When sleeping bags and bedrolls were properly packed, the group went to the auditorium for a song service and brief devotional. The most cooperative boys (chosen by the leaders as the kids prepared for bed the night before) got to set up tables and chairs for breakfast, and the most cooperative girls got to set the tables.

Breakfast was cereal and juice with the teachers and workers pouring the milk and juice. This eliminated spills and gave the workers the opportunity to serve the kids.

The second preaching service followed breakfast. Then came a final time of relay races and games, followed by the announcement of winning teams and awarding of ribbons.

The overnights were a lot of work and required a number of dedicated workers, but they were loads of fun. You should have seen the rapport that developed between teachers and pupils! The end result was this: our kids developed a fierce loyalty to Calvary Baptist Church. When approached by bus captains from other churches, most of them wouldn't even consider "visiting" for a Sunday. They knew that Calvary Baptist was the church where people loved them!

5. **Take your students on visitation and on errands with you.** When you take your students on visitation with you (and even on errands around town), you not only minister to the kids you are visiting, but also to the children who visit with you. Always be sure you have parental permission, and take at least two children with you at a time.

6. **Pray daily for your students.** Nothing draws the heart of the teacher to the students faster than spending time in prayer for them. Prayer deepens any relationship, and this is especially true in a teaching ministry. Do you want to develop a close, loving relationship with each of your students? Spend time in daily prayer for them!

Use your class roll book to call the names of each of your students in prayer. Pray for specific needs in their lives and in their families. Pray for their salvation, then their spiritual growth. Prayer will build a deep, lasting relationship.

I first met "Jeremy" one Sunday morning in Children's Church. I was pushing a wheelbarrow loaded with books across the floor as an illustration in my message. The wheel caught on an uneven place in the floor and flipped the wheelbarrow. I noticed a good-looking fourth-grade boy sitting on the front row, laughing scornfully. He actually pointed at me as he rudely laughed and continued to laugh

after the other kids had settled down.

Who is this kid? I thought to myself as I righted the wheelbarrow and continued with the message. *I've never seen a kid so hateful!*

To my dismay, two weeks later his family joined the church. Jeremy became one of the most disruptive kids in our ministry. He was arrogant and loud and loved to disrupt. He thrived on arguments and confrontations, and he'd just as soon take on a teacher as he would a fellow student. Within weeks, he had earned a reputation as a "bad kid," both in church and in our Christian day school. Sunday school teachers resented him, and I think he nearly drove his schoolteacher to a nervous breakdown.

At first, I deeply resented him. He seemed to delight in turning the Children's Church service into chaos. He was perhaps the most frustrating kid I have ever encountered, but I set out to win his heart. During the next twelve months, I took him and his younger sister somewhere at least once a week—hiking, errands, even visitation. To my surprise, when we were by ourselves, he was fun to be with! When he was in a group of kids, he always had a chip on his shoulder and seemed to have to prove himself; but when he was not around his peers, he was a really swell kid.

I learned not to confront his misbehavior in front of the group but to take him aside privately to deal with him. I would simply say, "Jeremy, there are lost kids here in Children's Church today, and I need your help. Instead of causing trouble and keeping these kids from hearing the Gospel, would you be praying for them?"

He'd respond soberly, "Okay, Mr. Dunlop. I'm sorry." For the rest of the hour, he'd be good as gold!

It took a long while, but by spending a good amount of time with him, praying for him, and proving to him that I really loved him, I won his trust and his love. We became close friends. I actually hated to see him enter Junior High and "graduate" from my Children's Church!

A year or two ago he called long distance from Florida to tell me that he was getting married and wanted to stop and see us on his honeymoon!

Love your students!

With a squeal of brakes, the bus rolled to a stop under a huge oak. Tim jumped to his feet. "Okay, gang, listen up! Mr. Perkins has the tractor and the wagons ready, and I think we're in for a fantastic hayride! Everyone, stay seated and listen to my directions.

"When we get off the bus, go straight to the hay wagons. The wagon closest to the tractor is the 'non-throwing' wagon; get on that one if you just want to ride in peace and don't like hay fights. The wagon in back is the 'throwing' wagon. Get on that one if you want to get in on some hay fights or want to try to stuff hay down Mr. Anderson's shirt. Once the ride starts, no one gets off the wagons for any reason.

"Ready? Let's ask the Lord for safety on the outing, then head for the wagons."

Tim laughed as he watched Lisa attempt to make her way to the hay wagons. She was surrounded by little girls and had so many of them hanging on her that she could hardly walk. "Lord, thank You for these kids," he softly breathed.

Ten-year-old Michael punched him playfully on the shoulder. "You coming on the throwing wagon, Mr. Wellington? I want to stuff hay down your shirt!"

Tim laughed and gently returned the punch. "Try it if you think you're big enough, Michael!" With a deep sense of satisfaction, he climbed up on the throwing wagon to join a group of laughing, scuffling boys and girls.

Developing close student/teacher relationships:
1. Call your students by name.
2. Listen when your students talk.
3. Visit in your students' homes.
4. Plan outings for your class.
5. Take your students on visitation and errands.
6. Pray daily for each student.

So, to be effective, you must...

Prepare.

Use visuals.

Reward good behavior.

Spruce up your classroom.

Teach with enthusiasm and excitement.

Captivate attention by using relevant stories.

Get your students participating in the program.

Get to know your students through home visitation.

Work to develop a close relationship with each student.

Building Relationships— How Am I Doing?

YES NO

1. Do I know each of my students by name?
2. Do I call them by name?
3. Do I have time for my students before and after class?
4. Do I listen when my students talk?
5. Have I visited in the home of every student?
6. Do I plan class outings regularly?
7. Do I enjoy being with my students?
8. Do I take students on visitation with me?
9. Do I take students on errands with me?
10. Do I invite them over to my house?
11. Do I pray for my students daily?
12. Do my students know me personally?
13. Do they trust me?
14. Do they share prayer requests and confidences with me?
15. Am I demonstrating the love of Christ to them?

Ask Andy!

Dear Andy,

We're just getting ready to start a Children's Church ministry at our church. How should we divide the age groups?

Penny Lofur

Dear Penny,

If you have enough qualified workers, place the Beginners (four- and five-year-olds) in one group, the Primaries (first through third grade) in another, and the Juniors (fourth through sixth grade) in the third class. It usually works to combine the Primaries and Juniors if you need to, but don't try to include the Beginners. It just doesn't work.

There's just too much difference in the needs, interests and attention spans of the Beginners, Primaries and Juniors to try to put them all together. Place the Beginners in their own class.

Andy

Dear Andy,

Is visitation really all that necessary? I run the King's Kids program at our church, and we have a talented staff of workers. We run a well-organized program and have a pretty good turnout each club night.

My workers have extremely busy schedules with the demands of jobs and families, school activities, sporting events, etc. I just can't bring myself to insist that they visit when our program is already running smoothly and attendance is good.

Sometimes I think we place too much emphasis on this visitation thing.

Will Power

Dear Will,

How can you get to know your students if you never visit in their homes? How can you minister to their needs if you don't really know them?

When you buy a new car, the dealer will try to sell you some options: CD player, rear air conditioning, tilt wheel, cruise control, etc. The options are nice, but they're not essential. You can drive without them. But some components of the car are not options; they are essentials: brakes, engine, transmission, etc. You can't drive without them!

Visitation is not a ministry option; it's one of the essentials!

Andy

10.
DEALING WITH DEFIANT DUDES (AND DUDESSES)

Daniel Anderson was drilling the memory verse, and most of the class was enthusiastically participating, but Lisa noticed a disturbance on the second row. She slipped quietly forward to investigate, and she found two girls struggling over the same seat.

"Girls!" she whispered. "What's going on?"

"She took my seat!" nine-year-old Miranda answered, fierceness in her voice. "I had to go to the bathroom, and when I got back, Leslie had my seat!"

"I did not!" Leslie shot back. "You're a little liar!"

"There's an empty seat beside you," Lisa pointed out. "Now, one of you slide over."

"Let her do it!" Miranda replied. "I was here first!"

"Liar!" Leslie had possession of most of the seat, and she had no intention of relinquishing it. She stuck her tongue out at Miranda, who promptly struck her in the face.

Lisa leaned over and grabbed Miranda by the arm before she could lash out again. "Come with me, Miranda," she whispered sternly.

Let's face it—in spite of all your preparation, prayer and planning,

Discipline problems will sometimes occur in any class.

discipline problems will still arise from time to time. You may have an exciting program with lots of variety and student participation, a captivating lesson with superb visuals, and a behavior contest that provides excellent motivation; and yet, somehow, the Devil will still manage to stir up trouble and distract your students from the gospel message.

When discipline problems arise, your response to them often determines not only how smoothly and effectively class will go that day, but also how often problems will arise in the future. Being a teacher requires the patience of Job, the wisdom of Solomon, and on occasion, the battle strategy of Joshua!

"**What you need to do,**" Larry suggested, "**is watch some other teachers in action. Watch how they handle discipline problems. You'll get some ideas as to what to do and even some ideas as to what not to do.**"

"**When would I do that?**" Tim said. "**We're busy with Children's Church every Sunday. If I go into the Sunday school classes, I'll just be a distraction because my kids are in those classes.**"

Larry shrugged. "**We have a kids' club program on Tuesday nights, 7:00 to 9:00. Why not come over and observe some of the different classes? Some of our teachers are outstanding, and then again, some are not so hot, but I think you'll get some good ideas.**"

Tim and Lisa stepped inside the door of the Faith Baptist Church educational building to be greeted by a pleasant woman in a smart-looking club uniform. "**Welcome,**" the woman warmly said. "**You're new here, aren't you?**" She glanced toward the door behind them as if expecting someone else to walk through. "**Do you have some children for our club?**"

Tim shook his head. "**We just came to observe. Where could we find Larry Edwards?**"

"**He's in charge of game time,**" the woman replied. "**You'll probably find him getting ready in the fellowship hall—third door on the right.**"

Larry was sorting a pile of beanbags and blindfolds by colors when Tim and Lisa found him. "I'm glad you came," he told them. "Club starts in about five minutes. I'll show you where to go."

They followed him down the hall, sidestepping groups of noisy kids heading to the various classes. Tim noticed that nearly every kid greeted Larry as he passed, and he responded to each with a friendly word, squeeze of the shoulder, or playful pull of a ponytail.

"The first and second graders have their Bible time first," he explained, "while the other age groups have their game time or Bible memory time. You can sit in on the first class and watch Mrs. Featherstone teach, then observe the other classes later in the evening."

Mrs. Featherstone was a middle-aged woman with a stern countenance. She led the class in three or four choruses, then launched into a Bible lesson. Within two minutes Tim realized that she was not properly prepared. Her lesson was on the raising of Lazarus, but she stumbled over the details of the story and had to search through a whole stack of flannelgraph figures every time she placed one on her board. The students soon grew restless.

"Young man," she declared, glaring sternly at one boy, "you have been talking ever since class started. If what you have to say is so important, perhaps you would like to share it with the whole class!"

The boy slumped in his seat, wilting under her fierce attention.

"Young man, I'm speaking to you! What's your name?"

"Timothy."

"Timothy, stand up."

Timothy timidly stood to his feet.

"Now, what was so important? I want you to share it with the rest of the class."

Head down, Timothy mumbled something and shook his head.

"Speak up, young man! We're waiting!" An uneasy silence reigned as Mrs. Featherstone towered over Timothy, hands on her hips, glaring at him fiercely.

"Mr. Evans," the teacher barked, "take Timothy out and let him sit in the hall. If he's going to be rude enough to talk in my class, he can just wait outside." She grabbed the unfortunate lad by the arm, spun him around, and marched him down the aisle toward Mr. Evans.

One of the girls let out a giggle, and Mrs. Featherstone pounced on her. "You too, young lady!" She grabbed the girl by the arm and jerked her from her seat, pinching the arm as she marched her toward the door. The little girl's eyes welled with tears as she was led from the room.

"Now, where were we?" Mrs. Featherstone managed a tight smile as she stepped in front of the class. An uncomfortable silence prevailed.

* * *

The fifth and sixth graders laughed and chattered as they filed into the classroom and took their seats. A thin-faced, balding man stepped to the front of the room. "Okay, time to start," he called. "Everyone, get quiet."

The noise continued.

"Get quiet!" The order was repeated with a little more emphasis and a lot more volume.

A few students grew quiet, but most continued talking.

The man slammed his Bible down on the desk with a WHACK! that made the students jump. "I'm not putting up with this," he said. "When I say 'quiet,' I mean quiet!"

A few students giggled, but most of the talking subsided.

A heavyset blond girl on the front row raised her hand. "Mr. Peabody?"

"Not now, Trina."

"But it's important."

The man sighed. "Okay, what is it?"

"I have to go to the bathroom." Several girls giggled.

"Not now, Trina. You should have gone before class."

"Well, I didn't, and I have to go now."

"I'm sorry, but you'll have to wait."

Trina made a face, turning in her seat so the other students could see her. "I have to go bad."

"I said no."

"Real bad."

Mr. Peabody waved a hand in exasperation. "Okay, okay, go, if it's such an emergency. Come back in quietly, and sit in the back so you don't disturb everyone."

Tim noticed that it took several more minutes for the class to get quiet enough to start, and that Mr. Peabody spent most of his time correcting problems instead of teaching, even though there were several other adults in the room. He also noticed that when Trina came back from the bathroom, she returned to her front row seat.

The teacher who is properly prepared will have a minimum of classroom interruptions and disturbances. But discipline problems will still arise from time to time, and it's important to handle them properly.

Here are a few tips to help things go more smoothly on those occasions when you are confronted with misbehavior in class:

1. **Seat your workers among the students.** There's just something about an adult worker in close proximity that squelches a lot of the misbehavior before it even has a chance to develop. Spot your workers at various points throughout the class, and instruct them to sing and participate along with the kids. Above all else, they should be praying.

If you allow your workers to congregate at the back of the room, they often tend to talk among themselves, even to the point of cutting up and becoming a distraction to the students.

Some ministries have their workers stand along the side walls during class, but this is still not the most effective. This tends to isolate the workers from the kids, creating a psychological barrier. Also, more of a distraction is created when a worker moves into the crowd to correct a problem.

It's always most effective to have your workers among the kids, participating in the activities and the message, praying and helping keep order.

2. **Train your workers to be alert to problems.** Even though your workers are praying and participating in the program, they need to be taught to be alert to everything that's

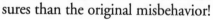

**BE ALERT!
(The world needs
more lerts.)**

taking place around them. When small problems of behavior arise, a worker can usually take care of the problem from where he is seated, and most of the class is not even aware of the distraction. When the teacher up front has to stop and correct a problem, everyone in class is aware of the interruption, and the distraction becomes major.

Many instances of misbehavior can be squelched simply with a stern look, a slight shake of the head, or a finger held briefly to the lips. If the child does not get the message, the worker needs to lean close or slip close to the child and verbally correct the situation in a very quiet voice. If the misbehavior continues or the situation warrants it, the worker should move the child to sit beside an adult worker at the back of the room.

3. **Be as unobtrusive as possible with your corrections.** Always remember that the goal is to have as few interruptions and distractions as possible, so that the attention of the class is at all times focused on the lesson. Often teachers create a bigger distraction with their corrective measures than the original misbehavior!

I used to direct a large Children's Church in Phoenix, Arizona. We had a young worker who would attempt to correct problems of behavior by grabbing the offender by an arm and a leg, hoisting the child over his head, and carrying him from the room! I'm sure that this method made an unforgettable impression upon the child in question, but it also created a major distraction every time he did it. I was quick to suggest milder, quieter ways of dealing with the kids, and my worker agreed to change his methods.

4. **Learn to "steal" the attention of the class away from the distractions.** When you see a distraction in the making (the department secretary coming forward to get the class offering envelope, a worker moving in on a troublesome kid, etc.), focus the attention of your class away from the disturbance by moving to the other side of the room and introducing a visual, using extremely large gestures, raising or lowering your voice, etc. It works! You'll be amazed at how many times you can "save" the flow of the lesson by being aware of what's going on in your class, anticipating the distractions before they start, and diverting the attention of your students away from the interruption or distraction.

5. **When misbehavior occurs, don't confront the offender in front of the group.** The child who purposely creates a disturbance in class is often seeking attention. Don't give it to him. When you go head-to-head with the offender in front of his peers, he's got to save face by standing up to you, and then the situation worsens. (It used to be that boys were confrontational and girls were usually submissive, but in today's society, the girls are as aggressive as the boys.)

If you correct a child and he (or she) becomes defiant, remove him from the room to deal with the misbehavior. Of course it's best for another worker to do it as quietly and unobtrusively as possible, rather than for the teacher up front to create a scene by doing it.

6. **Never embarrass or belittle a student in front of the group.** How many times I've seen teachers call down a student by name, then have the child stand as an example to the rest of the class! The teacher proceeds to scold the student publicly before allowing him or her to be reseated.

The student in question begins to resent you (and watches for future opportunities to "submarine" you), and the rest of the class often sees you as a bully.

A simple "Keisha, be seated, please,"

may be warranted, but never public embarrassment or humiliation.

7. Deal with the offender privately. It's always more effective for a worker to deal with the misbehaving child quietly outside or in the back of the room than to scold or berate the child before the entire class. You really want to talk and reason with the child, and this involves a two-way conversation. A private conference with the child affords you this opportunity.

8. **Use the child's name as you talk with him.** Be warm and friendly with the child as you talk with him. Use his name! You want to come across as a teacher who cares, not as a harsh disciplinarian who resents him.

9. **Be firm, but not harsh.** There's never any need to be harsh or hateful with a disorderly student. Be polite to the child, and speak in a gentle but firm voice. No matter how rude or obnoxious his behavior, there's no call to snarl at him, jerk him around, or show resentment toward him. When a teacher resents a student, the student is quick to pick up on it, and resentment builds toward the teacher.

Rather than displaying fleshly anger and resentment toward the troublesome child, ask God to allow you to respond as a Spirit-filled believer should respond, demonstrating the love of Christ. Anger and resentment damage your relationship with the student and accomplish nothing beneficial. Only as you allow the Holy Spirit to lead and guide you will you see the student begin to yield and his attitude begin to change.

Remember Proverbs 15:1: "A soft answer turneth away wrath: but grievous words stir up anger."

10. **Help the student to see your purpose.** As you talk with the child, deal with his misbehavior, but don't attack him as a person. Allow him to see that you love him, but that his behavior creates distractions

and keeps others from hearing the message.

Talk with him about his own salvation. Sometimes students act up because they are unsaved and fighting conviction. A discussion regarding misbehavior in class often leads into an opportunity to lead the child to Christ.

If you are sure that the child is saved, then explain to him that your purpose in class is to present the Gospel and help kids get saved, then teach them to live for Jesus. Gently point out that the child's misbehavior is a distraction and could possibly keep another child from hearing the message and being saved! Children seldom think through the consequences of their own misbehavior and are sometimes devastated and immediately repentant when they realize that they could keep another from the Saviour.

Use the question-and-answer method. Get the child talking and responding so that you may evaluate his attitude and know when you have gotten through to him.

If the child is repentant and a change of attitude is evident, pray with him, asking God to help him to do right in the future. Gently lead him to pray, asking God for forgiveness and help in doing right. Suggest that as he goes back to class, he should be praying for the students in class who are lost.

If the child is still rebellious and defiant, inform him of the action you plan to take (sending him to sit with his parents or bus captain, keeping him in the office, or in extreme cases, immediately taking him home). Whatever you do, don't allow him simply to return to his seat as if nothing had happened. There must be consequences for his actions.

11. **Return the child to the classroom but not to his original seat.** There are several reasons for this:

First, you don't need the additional distraction as the child marches back to his seat while the other students are watching to try to determine how the offender fared.

Second, the other students need to see that there were consequences, even if it's only being moved to the back row where visibility is not as good.

Third, the child (even the compliant, repentant one) will often assume an air of defiance as he takes his seat, merely to save face with his peers.

189

Fourth, should the child again misbehave, he should be in the back with the smallest possible audience.

The third- and fourth-grade girls stirred restlessly as Miss Driftwood droned on and on in a dull monotone. *She's not even using visuals*, Tim thought. *That would help some.* He took a deep breath and did his best to suppress a yawn.

The undercurrent of whispering and fidgeting increased. Miss Driftwood continued to try to teach, glaring from time to time at one particularly noisy girl or another. After a few minutes, she snapped her Bible closed.

"You are the rudest, most undisciplined group of kids that I have ever taught," she shrilled. "I'm ashamed of you! You don't listen! You don't care! You don't seem to have any respect whatsoever for the Word of God! I am trying to teach, and you all act like you're at a football game! Shame, shame, shame! If I were your parents..."

Tim leaned over to Lisa. "Let's get out of here," he whispered. "I don't think we're going to learn anything here."

* * *

Larry caught up with them in the hallway. "So, how's it going?" he asked. "Did you get the chance to observe the different classes?"

Tim frowned. "To be honest, Larry, we were a bit disappointed. These teachers didn't have their act together! Mrs. Featherstone wasn't really prepared, and she became almost abusive when discipline problems resulted. She was really rough on the kids, Larry. Mr. Peabody never did have control of his class, but his workers weren't involved in helping either. And Miss Driftwood just teaches along, letting the noise level build until she just can't stand it any longer, then she blows up at the class."

Larry nodded. "We have some staff problems, and we're getting ready to make some changes. We're gonna start a teacher-training series to give these people some help."

He turned and pointed down the hall. "Why don't you sit in on Mr. Teachmore's class? He's got the third- and fourth-grade boys, and he's an outstanding teacher. I think you'll learn some things from him."

Tim and Lisa quietly slipped into the back of the classroom to find a group of boys intently listening to a huge man with a friendly face and a broad smile. Mr. Teachmore taught with such energy and enthusiasm that Tim forgot all about observing the man's methods and was simply captivated by the lesson.

The man was teaching on the same passage that the other teachers had, the raising of Lazarus. But what a difference! Mr. Teachmore used his visual aids smoothly and effectively and told the story in such an interesting, intimate way that Tim got the impression that the man had known Mary and Martha personally. The students could actually feel the deep grief of the two sisters at the loss of their brother, then their overwhelming joy when they were reunited.

Tim finally remembered where he was and glanced around the room. Every boy was intently listening.

After a brief invitation, Mr. Teachmore addressed his students. "Mr. Davis is going to come and do our Bible game today! It's called 'Boomerang'! Which team is going to win—third grade or fourth?"

Mr. Davis came forward to introduce the Bible game, and Mr. Teachmore walked to the back of the room. One of the other workers met him. "We have a boy that's been causing quite a bit of trouble in Bible memory time, Will. Would you have the time to talk with him?"

The big man nodded. "Sure. Send him out to the drinking fountain."

Tim slipped from the room. Mr. Teachmore led a red-haired, freckle-faced boy to a lobby area near the drinking fountain, then sat down on a bench to talk with him. Tim loitered nearby, pretending to look at a missions bulletin board.

191

"You're Jason Walker, aren't you?" the big man said as he took a seat near the boy.

"Uh-huh." Jason's eyes were on the floor.

"My name is Mr. Teachmore. And I believe this is your third time at club, isn't it?"

"Uh-huh."

"Who do you come with, Jason?"

"Jimmy Hughes."

"Is he a neighbor?"

"He's in my class at school."

"Jason, do you like coming to club?"

"Uh-huh."

"What part of club do you like best?"

The boy thought for just a second. "Game time."

Mr. Teachmore's deep bass voice was warm and friendly. "What's your favorite game?"

Jason raised his head to look at Mr. Teachmore for the first time. "The four-way tug-of-war."

The big man laughed pleasantly. "That's a rough one, isn't it? But I like it too."

As Tim eavesdropped, Mr. Teachmore continued to talk with Jason in a gentle, friendly tone. Tim noticed that Jason began to relax and open up, answering Mr. Teachmore's questions in complete sentences rather than the tight-lipped, one- or two-word replies he had used at first. Before long, the two were chatting like old friends.

"I understand that you've been having some problems in Bible memory time, Jason." Mr. Teachmore's voice was still warm and kind, but firm.

Jason looked at the floor. "Yeah."

"Care to tell me about it?"

The boy shrugged. "Not really."

"Mr. Teamwork tells me that you talk out during Bible memory

192

time, cause distractions and even start fights. Is that true?"

Jason slowly nodded.

"Bible memory time is when we say handbook sections and work on learning new verses," Mr. Teachmore told him. "Have you been memorizing any Bible verses?"

Jason shook his head. "I don't have a book."

"Didn't Mr. Teamwork tell you how you could get one?"

"Yeah, but my mom says she's not buying one," Jason replied.

"Did she say why?" Mr. Teachmore questioned in a gentle voice.

"No, but I know why," the boy answered bitterly. "She wants to keep all her money for drugs and booze!"

At the bulletin board, Tim inwardly winced, sensing the hurt and disgust in Jason's voice.

"What if I buy you a handbook?" the big teacher offered. "Would you work on verses then?"

Jason was instantly suspicious. "Why would you do that," he questioned, "when my own mom won't buy me one?"

Mr. Teachmore's voice was husky-sounding as he answered. "We love you, Jason. And Jesus loves you. That's why we have this club for kids. We want to see kids get saved and then help them to live for Jesus. Memorizing Bible verses will help you live for Jesus, so I want to help you get your handbook."

Jason was quiet as he thought it over. "If you buy me a book, I'll start learning the verses," he said quietly.

"It's a deal," Mr. Teachmore replied. "We'll get your book tonight."

He turned to look the boy directly in the eye. "Do you understand why it's so important to follow directions and listen in handbook time? We're trying to teach you and the other boys how to be saved and live for Jesus and have happy lives. We have the Bible lesson time for the same reasons, but if you talk and cut up, you keep other boys from hearing the message."

Jason was silent.

"I'm glad you're coming to our club," Mr. Teachmore went on.

"I hope you'll keep coming. Maybe someday we can get your mom to come to church too."

"Don't hold your breath," Jason muttered. Mr. Teachmore ignored his comment.

"Jason, you don't want to keep other kids from hearing about Jesus, do you?"

The boy shook his head.

"Do you see why it's so important to listen and follow the rules and make sure you're not distracting other kids? I want to ask you to help by listening and being quiet when you're supposed to. You can help me and help the other kids in that way, but if you talk and break the rules and fight, you're not helping, are you?"

To Tim's surprise, Jason suddenly seemed to wilt. His shoulders slumped as he whispered hoarsely, "I'm sorry, Mr. Teachmore."

The big man put a gentle hand on the boy's shoulder. "Jason, let me ask you this: have you ever asked Jesus to be your Saviour? We've been talking about it the last few weeks in club..."

Tim prayed as he quietly slipped back into the classroom.

Dealing With Discipline Problems

1. Seat your workers among the students.
2. Train your workers to be alert to problems.
3. Handle problems as unobtrusively as possible.
4. Learn to divert attention away from distractions.
5. Don't confront troublemakers in front of the group.
6. Never embarrass or belittle a student.
7. Deal privately with the offender.
8. Use the child's name as you talk with him/her.
9. Be firm, but not harsh.
10. Help the student to see your purpose.
11. Don't return the child to his/her original seat.

So, to be effective, you must...

Prepare.

Use visuals.

Reward good behavior.

Spruce up your classroom.

Teach with enthusiasm and excitement.

Captivate attention by using relevant stories.

Get your students participating in the program.

Get to know your students through home visitation.

Work to develop a close relationship with each student.

Learn how to deal with discipline problems when they arise.

Perry Pedagogue

Last week I told Pastor that I was going to quit teaching 'cus I couldn't get my girls to stop talking in class.

He told me that I needed to "stick with it."

His choice of words gave me a great idea!

How Well Do We Handle Discipline Problems?

YES NO

1. Our workers sit among the kids, always participating and praying.
2. Our workers are alert and quickly respond to problems around them.
3. We quietly and unobtrusively as possible deal with behavior problems.
4. We don't confront the offender in front of the group.
5. We never attempt to embarrass or belittle a student.
6. We deal privately with the offenders.
7. We always address the children by name.
8. We know how to be firm, but not harsh.
9. We demonstrate the love of Christ to the student, even when dealing with problems of misbehavior.
10. We never show hostility or resentment.
11. We use the question-and-answer method to get the student talking.
12. We attempt to let the student see our purpose for teaching.
13. We explain to the student how his/her misbehavior disrupts and distracts others.
14. When the offender is repentant, we lead him/her in a prayer of confession.
15. When the offender is defiant, we gently take the necessary action.
16. We don't return the offender to his/her original seat.

Ask Andy!

Dear Andy,

We have a child in our department who must be hyperactive. I don't think she can sit still for two minutes. She wiggles and squirms, plays with her clothing, nudges the kids around her, etc., etc., etc.

She's been coming for nearly a year, and we've actually seen some improvement in her behavior. She can be quite distracting to the other students, but we think she's really trying, so we hate to tell her she can't come.

Do you have any suggestions that might improve the situation? This girl can be quite a handful, but we do want to minister to her.

Rose Bush

Dear Rose,

I appreciate your desire to minister to this troublesome child.

Do your best to minimize any distractions that she might cause. I would suggest seating her behind the other students, at the outside end of the row, with a worker right beside her.

Do your best to minister to this girl, but don't allow her to hinder other children from hearing the message.

Andy

Dear Andy,

We have three boys from one of our bus routes that always

198

insist on sitting together in Children's Church, but when they do, they always cause trouble!

Any suggestions?

Ray Gunn

Dear Ray,

Don't allow these boys to sit together; move them to the locations where they can cause the least trouble, but tell them why you're moving them. You might consider offering them the privilege of sitting together again the following week if they can go through the entire service without causing any distractions. Then let them know that if they mess up just once when they are seated together, you will immediately move them. Make sure they understand that sitting together is a privilege, not a right.

If they continue to cause trouble after you have given them a few chances, simply refuse to allow them to sit together at all.

Andy

11.

THE POWER OF PREVAIL-
ING PRAYER

A tormented scream cut through the noisy confusion of the crowded marketplace. Fear swept across the crowd as mothers frantically hurried their terrified children away from the danger; shopkeepers shuttered their windows and bolted their doors. "The evil one has returned," a hoarse voice muttered in apprehension.

The horrified crowd watched in silence as the screaming young man fell writhing to the ground. Foaming at the mouth, he snarled and howled and cursed as his body thrashed and flopped in fearful convulsions. The awestruck masses kept their distance, frightened by the animal-like shrieks and wails. A few of the braver souls crept closer as their curiosity got the best of them.

Suddenly the youth leaped to his feet, eyes wide with torment, screaming and spewing a vile liquid from his mouth. The spectators quickly moved back. Snarling with rage, the boy dashed through the crowd to hurl himself into the blazing fire in front of the coppersmith's shop. The crowd gasped with horror as sparks flew in all directions.

"No, no, dear God, no!" a green-robed man shouted in anguish as he plunged through the crowd to seize the back of the boy's coat. Grunting with the effort, he jerked the young man's body from the fire, then beat out the flames with his own headgear. The young man's hair was singed, but, miraculously, he seemed unhurt.

He lay motionless on the ground, eyes wide but unseeing. The man bent over him.

With the cry of a wounded animal, the youth hurled the man to one side, then leaped to his feet. Screaming and crying, he dashed wildly down the street. The crowd followed at a distance.

The sound of a heavy splash told the throng that the wild boy had leaped into the river. The man in the green robe was frantic. "No!" he shouted. "No, David, you must not do this! You must live!"

He waded into the shallow water at the river's edge where the young man's body was visible beneath the water as he thrashed and struggled. Voices murmured in fear as the crowd viewed the spectacle. It was as though an unseen force were dragging the young man beneath the surface.

The frantic man struggled to pull the body from the water. He lifted an imploring face to the crowd on the bank above. "Help me!" he pleaded. "Somebody, help me!"

Two burly men jumped into the shallows and seized the young man's clothing. Together they struggled to drag him from the water. Moments later, the youth lay unconscious on the riverbank, the man in green bending over him in concern.

Someone in the crowd laid a gentle hand on his shoulder. "Help is on the way. The disciples of Jesus are coming."

The crowd parted in respect and reverence as the tall figures of Peter, James, John and Andrew strode purposefully toward the river. The husky frame of Simon Peter cast a shadow across the prostrate form on the ground as he raised one hand heavenward. "In the name of Jesus Christ of Nazareth," Peter's bass voice thundered, "I command you to come out of this lad!"

The boy's eyes jerked open. Quicker than the eye could follow, he leaped to his feet and threw his small frame directly at the impressive hulk of Peter, striking him squarely in the chest. To the astonishment of the crowd, Peter was sent tumbling!

The boy dashed up the riverbank toward the crowd. His body suddenly went limp, and he slumped to the ground. A low moan issued from his throat.

"The worst is over for now," the man in the green robe told Simon Peter, who had brushed himself off and now leaned over them in concern. "He'll be like this for an hour or so, then be back to his normal self for awhile. But can't you do something?"

Peter scratched his head. "We tried," he answered. "We really did. But there's nothing more we can do for him. Is he kin to you?"

The older man's eyes filled with tears. "He's my son," he whispered.

"Jesus is teaching in the next village," Peter told him. "Let's take your son to Him."

Thirty minutes later, Jesus leaned over the unconscious form of the boy. "Lord, can you help us?" the father begged. "This evil spirit is about to destroy my son. I brought him to Your disciples, but they couldn't do anything!"

Jesus turned and looked at the man kindly. "If thou canst believe," He said, "all things are possible to him that believeth."

"Lord, I believe!" the man said with tears streaming down his face. "Please help my unbelief!"

When Jesus commanded the demon to leave the youth, a shrill scream rent the air. The boy rose to his feet but then was slammed to the ground with such force that the bystanders thought he had been killed. Jesus took him by the hand and lifted him up, then presented him to a grateful father. "Your son lives," He said. "Your faith is rewarded."

Later that evening, the perplexed disciples gathered around Jesus. "Why couldn't we cast the demon out?" Peter asked. "We commanded him in Your name, as You taught us to. But the demon refused to obey. Why?"

We should never forget the answer that Jesus gave the disciples: "This kind can come forth by nothing," He said, "but by prayer and fasting."

Tim and Larry knelt side by side at the Wellingtons' faded blue sofa. Across the room, Lisa and Debbie also knelt together. "Lord, we're looking forward to tomorrow," Tim prayed, "as we teach Your Word to several dozen boys and girls. Thank You, thank You, for entrusting Debbie and me with such a blessed privilege.

"We ask that You fill us with Your power and Your Spirit as we teach. In Jesus' name we ask that You defeat Satan as he tries to hinder the ministry of Your Word. Please don't allow him to create distractions and disturbances to keep the kids from hearing the Gospel. Don't allow him to come and snatch away the seed as it is

planted. We ask that You protect the service.

"Father, I ask that You settle the hearts of my students. Give us a good service. May it be enjoyable and exciting, and help the kids to enjoy being there. I ask right now that You prepare the heart of each and every child for the message from Your Word. Help the kids to listen. Give me the words to speak so that every student will listen and understand the message. Please give me the full attention of every kid.

"I thank You for Larry and how he's been teaching me the importance of prayer. Bless him and Debbie and the rest of their crew as they teach their own group of kids. Have Your way in their service as well, and may souls be saved tomorrow.

"And, Lord, I pray for Rusty. We're not sure he's saved, Lord, but he…" A sob cut off his words. He wiped his eyes with the back of his hand and took a deep breath.

A tear trickled down Larry's cheek as Tim continued to pray for his students by name, asking God to save them and change their lives.

I saved this chapter for last—-not because it's the least important, but rather, to emphasize its importance. As you finish reading this book, I trust that one thought will stay with you: **The most vital aspect of your ministry to children is your ministry of prayer.**

Prayer is essential. Prayer is vital. Nothing of eternal value will ever be accomplished without prayer. The world's finest teacher might prepare an exciting program, plan a captivating lesson with the finest visuals, and deliver a flawless presentation with vibrant enthusiasm, yet see it fail for lack of prayer.

We must never forget that we are engaged in spiritual warfare and that teaching the Word of God engages us in the fiercest of battles. Do you not realize that the enemy knows how to create diversions and distractions in your class for the very purpose of hindering the presentation of the Scripture? Do you not realize that the Devil himself is the source of much of the misbehavior and disorder in class? How can we ever hope to win against his forces without using the mighty weapon of prayer?

PRAYER

may very well be the most important facet of your entire ministry.

A teacher who fails to pray is like a soldier without ammunition, a firefighter without equipment, or a guide without map or compass. He's a doctor without medicine, a musician without music, an artist with no brush.

How many times I've stood to teach or preach when the kids were restless and disorderly, the message seemed to fall flat, and there were no results. Only after the teaching hour was over did I realize that I had not spent the time in prayer that I needed!

Prayer is absolutely essential to any children's ministry. A ministry without prayer is simply an exercise in futility.

Pray for your class. Make it a habit to spend much time in prayer throughout the week as you prepare for class. Pray that the elements of your program will go smoothly; pray for God's power and blessing on the lesson; pray for God's leading in the invitation. Bathe your teaching ministry in prayer.

Pray for your students. Use your class roll book as a prayer list and bring each student by name before God. Pray for specific needs and problems; pray for their family situations. Pray for the salvation of lost students and for growth and victory for the saved. This is perhaps the most essential aspect of your entire ministry. Pray!

Take advantage of those "wasted" moments to pray for your class. That twenty-minute drive to work is an excellent time for prayer. When you're waiting in the doctor's office or for your appointment at the hair dresser's, use the time to pray. When you stand in line at the checkout in the grocery store, don't waste the time scanning the ridiculous headlines on the tabloids; use the time to pray for your class!

Before you step into class, confess any known sin and make sure that your heart is right with God. Sin will not only hinder your prayer life, it will also make you ineffective as a teacher and keep God from using you.

Open class with prayer. Many times teachers open class with prayer as a mere formality. Pray from your heart! Ask God to guide you as you teach, to give you the words to say that your students will listen to and that your students will understand the message of the Scriptures. Ask Him to help your students to be orderly and attentive. Pray for the salvation of any in the class who are lost. Commit your class to the Lord every time you teach.

I never stand to teach or preach without asking God for two things: that He give me the full attention of every person present, and that He help each student to understand the message *fully*.

Pray as you teach. The teacher must be in constant communion with God as he teaches, depending upon Him for guidance and power. If you sense a growing restlessness during the lesson, ask God to rekindle the interest of your students toward the lesson. When you see a distraction just about to take place, ask God to divert it and protect your lesson presentation. Depend on the Lord to keep order and hold the attention of your pupils. Never attempt to teach in your own power!

I remember conducting a drug and alcohol assembly in a public junior high school in North Carolina. As hundreds of students filed into the gymnasium before the assembly, I realized that I was about to face one of the roughest groups of students I had ever encountered. I prayed in desperation, committing the situation to the Lord and asking for His power. The students actually mocked the principal as he began my introduction, and I knew we were headed for trouble.

But to my amazement, a hush came over the crowd as I stood to speak! The Holy Spirit took charge of that presentation, and *He* captivated the entire crowd. It was one of the most effective assemblies I have ever had. Teachers commented afterward that they had never seen their students so quiet and attentive.

Teach your workers to pray during class. Your assistants and workers can be effective prayer warriors as they hold you and the students up in prayer during class. So often it never even occurs to them unless you instruct them to do so!

The duties of an assistant:

1. Pray.
2. Sit among the kids.
3. Help keep order.
4. Pray.
5. Sing and participate.
6. Pray.
7. Anticipate problems.
8. Pray.
9. Help with details.
10. Pray.

As I write this, I am preaching at a Junior camp with over three hundred Juniors. The counselors and staff are students from the better Christian colleges around the nation. But as I preach this week, I sense that very few of them are praying! Many of the staff sit in the back and cut up during the service! If only they could see their responsibility to pray and realize the tremendous things that could be accomplished in the lives of these Juniors if only they would pray!

Ask godly parents to pray. Many times your best prayer warriors will be people who are not even directly involved in your ministry. The parents of your students have a vested interest in your ministry—you are teaching their children. Approach some of them and ask them to remember your teaching ministry in prayer. Some will undoubtedly take it lightly, but others will become serious prayer partners with you; they will pray for you as they sit in their own classes or services.

Again, one of the most effective ways to have an attentive, orderly class that listens and responds is to ask God for it. Pray! The most vital facet of your ministry is fervent prayer. Without prayer, the most talented teacher in the world is doomed to failure.

"Father, I just want to thank You for calling Lisa and me to teach in Children's Church," Tim prayed. "These past few weeks have been the most blessed time of our lives! We love our kids, and we love the ministry of teaching them. Again we simply ask You to use us to reach each of our kids for You. Thank You, Lord, for allowing us to teach. We love it! In Jesus' name. Amen."

"Amen," Larry whispered.

So, to be effective, you must...

Prepare.

Use visuals.

Reward good behavior.

Spruce up your classroom.

Teach with enthusiasm and excitement.

Captivate attention by using relevant stories.

Get your students participating in the program.

Get to know your students through home visitation.

Work to develop a close relationship with each student.

Learn how to deal with discipline problems when they arise.

Claim God's power by praying over *every detail* of your ministry.

Evaluating My Prayer Ministry

YES NO

__ __ 1. Do I know each of my students by name?

__ __ 2. Do I pray for each student by name weekly? daily?

__ __ 3. Do my students know that I pray for them?

__ __ 4. Do they trust me enough to share intimate prayer requests with me?

__ __ 5. Do I visit in the homes of my students so that I am familiar with their backgrounds and needs?

__ __ 6. Do I walk with God?

__ __ 7. Is my heart completely yielded to and right with God and free from unconfessed sin?

__ __ 8. Do I pray throughout the process of lesson preparation?

__ __ 9. Do I earnestly pray as I begin class?

__ __ 10. Do I silently pray when facing problems of misbehavior and inattention?

__ __ 11. Do my workers pray during class?

__ __ 12. Do I pray "overtime" for my troublesome students?

__ __ 13. Do I see prayer as the most important facet of my ministry?

A FINAL WORD

Tim's heart was overflowing as he strolled down the glittering boulevard. He had just come from spending time in the very presence of his Saviour. A deep sigh of contentment escaped his lips. What joy he had experienced being with Jesus!

He glanced up to notice that he was passing some particularly magnificent mansions. *I must be in one of the most beautiful sections of the city,* he told himself. He paused for a moment, soaking in the beauty and grandeur around him.

The front door of one of the mansions opened, and a lovely little girl dashed toward him. "Mr. Wellington!" she called. "Wait for me!"

With a cry of delight, she threw herself into his arms, and he hugged her tightly. "Jessica! How good to see you here!"

"I'm here because of you," she answered brightly. "You were the one who told me about Jesus!" She hugged him again.

Another girl whom Tim had never met joined them, but Tim knew her instantly. "You must be Samantha," he said, as she hugged him.

"Samantha is here because of you too," Jessica told him, "because after I got saved, I showed her how to get saved."

Several children strolled toward them and then, recognizing Tim, ran to meet him with hugs of joy. His eyes welled with tears as he realized that they were all children who had been saved as a result of his Children's Church ministry.

The happy group grew larger and larger as more children joined them. Some were children whom Tim had personally won; others had been saved as a result of the witness of those kids. Tears of joy flowed as there was one happy reunion after another. Before long, the joyful group around Tim numbered in the hundreds, including some adults and teens.

Tim looked about in astonishment. *Lisa and I only had a few years together in Children's Church,* he thought. *I never dreamed that we could have influenced this many lives!*

A tall man strode toward the group, and Tim recognized him. "You're Andrew," he said with awe, "one of Jesus' twelve apostles."

"And you're Brother Timothy, the man who reached so many children for our Saviour," Andrew answered, embracing him in a fierce hug. "Welcome to the City of the Redeemed!"

He looked over the crowd of happy children. "Are these your sheaves?" he asked. "You had quite a harvest for the Master!"

Tim joyfully nodded. "I never imagined," he told the tall apostle, "that Lisa and I could ever reach so many souls through our Children's Church ministry. But here they are! We personally led some of these to Jesus, and they reached others, and then those reached..." His voice trailed off as he was overcome with emotion.

Andrew laughed and nodded. "It was that way for me too. When I brought my brother Simon to Jesus, I had no idea of the immensity of what was going to happen. As you know, Simon reached multitudes for the Master."

Tim looked about him. "You know," he told Andrew, "I just realized that here there are no cars or motorcycles or investment portfolios or any of those things that seemed so important down on earth."

Andrew shook his head. "Just souls," he replied. "Just souls. That's all that really matters."

"Thank God that He used me to reach these souls!" Tim said, rejoicing. He looked over the throng of rejoicing children in their shimmering white robes, and a somber thought hit him. A tear glistened in his eye as he turned back to Andrew.

"I just wish," he said softly, "that I had reached more."

Lisa leaned over him. "Tim, what's wrong? You're crying!"

"I wish I had reached more," Tim sobbed. "I wish I had given my all and we had reached more!"

"More what, Sweetheart?" Lisa questioned. "What are you talking about?"

Tim opened his eyes. Waves of disappointment swept over him as he realized that Heaven had been just a dream.

"I was in Heaven," he told Lisa, "and there were hundreds of children around me—children that you and I had reached through our Children's Church ministry! And kids whom our kids had won!

"Lisa, you should have seen them! They were so happy! And then I saw Andrew, Simon Peter's brother, and we were talking about how that the only thing that matters in eternity is the souls we reach for Jesus."

He hugged her tightly. "Lisa, we've got to give our best every day! There are so many more kids we can reach for the Lord, and time is so short! We must reach more!"

He lay back down, and a deep sigh escaped him. "The dream was so real! I wish you could have seen the kids!"

ABOUT THE AUTHOR

"How Do I Get These Kids to Listen?" is the result of twenty-five years of Children's Church ministry. Ed Dunlop taught in Primary Church for three years and directed Junior Churches for thirteen years before going into children's evangelism full-time in March of 1988. In his traveling ministry he has spoken in scores of Children's Churches in twenty-six states.

A graduate of Pacific Coast Baptist Bible College, Ed holds memberships in the *North American Association of Ventriloquists* and the *Fellowship of Christian Magicians.* His ministry includes ventriloquism, balloon sculpturing, blacklight effects, and a VARIETY of other visual media. He and his family travel most of the year, presenting Kids' Crusades in churches, speaking at junior camps, and conducting drug/alcohol assemblies in the public schools.

Ed writes magazine articles, gospel tracts, and adventure books for middle readers. His other books for teachers include *Overhead Projector Games* and *More! Overhead Projector Games, Teaching With Bible Games, Let's Play a Bible Game!* and *"I Can't Wait Till Sunday Morning!"*

Ed and his wife, Janice, make their home in northern Georgia. They have three children, Rebecca, Steve and Phillip.

Ed says, "Your children's ministry is important to God! Ask Him to help you to always give your very best!"

For a complete list of books available from the Sword of the Lord, write to Sword of the Lord Publishers, P. O. Box 1099, Murfreesboro, Tennessee 37133.

(800) 247-9673
(615) 893-6700
FAX (615) 848-6943